JAMES M. KOUZES | BARRY Z. POSNER

Student Leadership Practices Inventory

SECOND EDITION

[OBSERVER]

Student Leadership Practices Inventory

by James M. Kouzes | Barry Z. Posner

[OBSERVER]

INSTRUCTIONS

On the next two pages are thirty statements describing various leadership behaviors. Please read each statement carefully. Then **rate the person who asked you to complete this form** about *how frequently* he or she engages in the behavior described. *This is not a test* (there are no right or wrong answers).

Consider each statement in the context of a student organization with which the person you are describing is most involved with or with which you have had the greatest opportunity to observe him or her. This organization could be a club, team, chapter, group, unit, hall, program, project, and the like. Maintain a *consistent* organizational perspective as you respond to each statement. The rating scale provides five choices:

1 If this person RARELY or SELDOM does what is described

2 If this person does what is described ONCE IN A WHILE

3 If this person SOMETIMES does what is described

4 If this person OFTEN does what is described

5 If this person VERY FREQUENTLY or ALMOST ALWAYS does what is described

- Be realistic about the extent to which this person actually engages in the behavior.
- Be as honest and accurate as you can be.
- *Do not* answer in terms of how you would like this person to behave or in terms of how you or someone else might think the person should behave.
- *Do* answer in terms of how this person typically engages on most days, on most projects, with most people.
- Be thoughtful about your responses; giving all fives or all threes or all ones is most likely not an accurate description. Most people will do some things more or less often than they do other things.
- If you feel a statement does not apply, it's probably because you don't observe this person engaging in the behavior; and, in that case, simply circle the number 1.
- Please respond to every statement.

For each statement, decide on a response and then circle the corresponding number to the right of the statement. For example, the first statement is "This person sets a personal example of what he or she expects from other people." If you believe the person does this *once in a while*, circle the number 2. If you believe the person sets a personal example of what he or she expects from others fairly *often*, circle the number 4. Select and circle only one option (response number) for each statement.

When you have responded to all thirty statements, please turn to the response sheet on the back page and transfer your responses as instructed.

Name of the individual whom you are thinking about in responding to these statements: _____

How frequently does this person *typically* engage in the following behaviors and actions? *Circle* the number to the right of each statement, using the scale below, that best applies.

1	2	3	4	5
RARELY OR SELDOM	ONCE IN A WHILE	SOMETIMES	OFTEN	VERY FREQUENTLY

1.	Sets a personal example of what he or she expects from other people.	1	2	3	4	5
2.	Looks ahead and communicates about what he or she believes will affect us in the future.	1	2	3	4	5
3.	Looks for ways to develop and challenge people's skills and abilities.	1	2	3	4	5
4.	Fosters cooperative rather than competitive relationships among people he or she works with.	1	2	3	4	5
5.	Praises people for a job well done.	1	2	3	4	5
6.	Spends time making sure that people behave consistently with the principles and standards that have been agreed upon.	1	2	3	4	5
7.	Describes to others in the organization what we should be capable of accomplishing.	1	2	3	4	5
8.	Looks for ways that others can try out new ideas and methods.	1	2	3	4	5
9.	Actively listens to diverse points of view.	1	2	3	4	5
10.	Encourages others as they work on activities and programs.	1	2	3	4	5
11.	Follows through on the promises and commitments he or she makes.	1	2	3	4	5
12.	Talks with others about a vision of how things could be even better in the future.	1	2	3	4	5
13.	Searches for innovative ways to improve what is being done.	1	2	3	4	5
14.	Treats others with dignity and respect.	1	2	3	4	5
15.	Expresses appreciation for the contributions that people make.	1	2	3	4	5
16.	Seeks to understand how his or her actions affect other people's performance.	1	2	3	4	5
17.	Talks with others about how their own interests can be met by working toward a common goal.	1	2	3	4	5
18.	When things do not go as he or she expected, asks, "What can we learn from this experience?"	1	2	3	4	5
19.	Supports the decisions that other people make on their own.	1	2	3	4	5
20.	Makes it a point to publicly recognize people who show commitment to shared values.	1	2	3	4	5
21.	Makes sure that people support the values that have been agreed upon.	1	2	3	4	5
22.	Is upbeat and positive when talking about what could be accomplished.	1	2	3	4	5
23.	Makes sure that big projects undertaken are broken down into smaller and doable parts.	1	2	3	4	5
24.	Gives others a great deal of freedom and choice in deciding how to do their work.	1	2	3	4	5
25.	Finds ways for people to celebrate accomplishments.	1	2	3	4	5
26.	Talks about his or her values and the principles that guide his or her actions.	1	2	3	4	5
27.	Speaks with passion about the higher purpose and meaning of what is being done.	1	2	3	4	5
28.	Takes initiative in experimenting with the way things can be done.	1	2	3	4	5
29.	Provides opportunities for others to take on leadership responsibilities.	1	2	3	4	5
30.	Makes sure that people are creatively recognized for their contributions.	1	2	3	4	5

TRANSFERRING THE RESPONSES

After you have responded to the thirty statements on the previous page, please transfer your responses to the blanks below. This will make it easier to record and score your responses.

Notice that the numbers of the statements are listed *horizontally* across the page. Make sure that the number you assigned to each statement is transferred to the appropriate blank. Remember to fill in a response option (1, 2, 3, 4, 5) for every statement.

1. _____	2. _____	3. _____	4. _____	5. _____
6. _____	7. _____	8. _____	9. _____	10. _____
11. _____	12. _____	13. _____	14. _____	15. _____
16. _____	17. _____	18. _____	19. _____	20. _____
21. _____	22. _____	23. _____	24. _____	25. _____
26. _____	27. _____	28. _____	29. _____	30. _____

If the name of the person who asked you to complete the Student LPI-Observer is not written below or on the first page, please add it yourself:_____

FURTHER INSTRUCTIONS

You should have received instructions to:

☐ Bring this page with you to the class (seminar or workshop) or

☐ Return this form to:

_____

_____

_____

_____

For more information on The Student LPI and *The Student Leadership Challenge*, including books, workbooks, and other learning materials, go to www.studentleadershipchallenge.com.

Copyright © 2013 by James M. Kouzes and Barry Z. Posner. All rights reserved.
Published by Jossey-Bass
A Wiley Imprint
1 Montgomery, Suite 1200, San Francisco, CA 94104 www.jossey-bass.com/highereducation

To contact Jossey-Bass directly call our Customer Care Department within the U.S. at 800–956–7739, outside the U.S. at 317–572–3986, or fax 317–572–4002.

ISBN 978-0-7879-8030-6

ISBN10: 0–7879–8030-7, ISBN13: 978–07879–8030–6
Printed in the United States of America
Printing 20 19 18 17 16 15 14 13 12

JAMES M. KOUZES | BARRY Z. POSNER

Student Leadership
Practices Inventory

SECOND EDITION

[OBSERVER]

Student Leadership Practices Inventory

by James M. Kouzes | Barry Z. Posner

[OBSERVER]

INSTRUCTIONS

On the next two pages are thirty statements describing various leadership behaviors. Please read each statement carefully. Then **rate the person who asked you to complete this form** about *how frequently* he or she engages in the behavior described. *This is not a test* (there are no right or wrong answers).

Consider each statement in the context of a student organization with which the person you are describing is most involved with or with which you have had the greatest opportunity to observe him or her. This organization could be a club, team, chapter, group, unit, hall, program, project, and the like. Maintain a *consistent* organizational perspective as you respond to each statement. The rating scale provides five choices:

1 If this person RARELY or SELDOM does what is described

2 If this person does what is described ONCE IN A WHILE

3 If this person SOMETIMES does what is described

4 If this person OFTEN does what is described

5 If this person VERY FREQUENTLY or ALMOST ALWAYS does what is described

- Be realistic about the extent to which this person actually engages in the behavior.
- Be as honest and accurate as you can be.
- *Do not* answer in terms of how you would like this person to behave or in terms of how you or someone else might think the person should behave.
- *Do* answer in terms of how this person typically engages on most days, on most projects, with most people.
- Be thoughtful about your responses; giving all fives or all threes or all ones is most likely not an accurate description. Most people will do some things more or less often than they do other things.
- If you feel a statement does not apply, it's probably because you don't observe this person engaging in the behavior; and, in that case, simply circle the number 1.
- Please respond to every statement.

For each statement, decide on a response and then circle the corresponding number to the right of the statement. For example, the first statement is "This person sets a personal example of what he or she expects from other people." If you believe the person does this *once in a while*, circle the number 2. If you believe the person sets a personal example of what he or she expects from others fairly *often*, circle the number 4. Select and circle only one option (response number) for each statement.

When you have responded to all thirty statements, please turn to the response sheet on the back page and transfer your responses as instructed.

Name of the individual whom you are thinking about in responding to these statements: _____

How frequently does this person *typically* engage in the following behaviors and actions? *Circle* the number to the right of each statement, using the scale below, that best applies.

1	2	3	4	5
RARELY OR SELDOM	ONCE IN A WHILE	SOMETIMES	OFTEN	VERY FREQUENTLY

1.	Sets a personal example of what he or she expects from other people.	1	2	3	4	5
2.	Looks ahead and communicates about what he or she believes will affect us in the future.	1	2	3	4	5
3.	Looks for ways to develop and challenge people's skills and abilities.	1	2	3	4	5
4.	Fosters cooperative rather than competitive relationships among people he or she works with.	1	2	3	4	5
5.	Praises people for a job well done.	1	2	3	4	5
6.	Spends time making sure that people behave consistently with the principles and standards that have been agreed upon.	1	2	3	4	5
7.	Describes to others in the organization what we should be capable of accomplishing.	1	2	3	4	5
8.	Looks for ways that others can try out new ideas and methods.	1	2	3	4	5
9.	Actively listens to diverse points of view.	1	2	3	4	5
10.	Encourages others as they work on activities and programs.	1	2	3	4	5
11.	Follows through on the promises and commitments he or she makes.	1	2	3	4	5
12.	Talks with others about a vision of how things could be even better in the future.	1	2	3	4	5
13.	Searches for innovative ways to improve what is being done.	1	2	3	4	5
14.	Treats others with dignity and respect.	1	2	3	4	5
15.	Expresses appreciation for the contributions that people make.	1	2	3	4	5
16.	Seeks to understand how his or her actions affect other people's performance.	1	2	3	4	5
17.	Talks with others about how their own interests can be met by working toward a common goal.	1	2	3	4	5
18.	When things do not go as he or she expected, asks, "What can we learn from this experience?"	1	2	3	4	5
19.	Supports the decisions that other people make on their own.	1	2	3	4	5
20.	Makes it a point to publicly recognize people who show commitment to shared values.	1	2	3	4	5
21.	Makes sure that people support the values that have been agreed upon.	1	2	3	4	5
22.	Is upbeat and positive when talking about what could be accomplished.	1	2	3	4	5
23.	Makes sure that big projects undertaken are broken down into smaller and doable parts.	1	2	3	4	5
24.	Gives others a great deal of freedom and choice in deciding how to do their work.	1	2	3	4	5
25.	Finds ways for people to celebrate accomplishments.	1	2	3	4	5
26.	Talks about his or her values and the principles that guide his or her actions.	1	2	3	4	5
27.	Speaks with passion about the higher purpose and meaning of what is being done.	1	2	3	4	5
28.	Takes initiative in experimenting with the way things can be done.	1	2	3	4	5
29.	Provides opportunities for others to take on leadership responsibilities.	1	2	3	4	5
30.	Makes sure that people are creatively recognized for their contributions.	1	2	3	4	5

TRANSFERRING THE RESPONSES

After you have responded to the thirty statements on the previous page, please transfer your responses to the blanks below. This will make it easier to record and score your responses.

Notice that the numbers of the statements are listed *horizontally* across the page. Make sure that the number you assigned to each statement is transferred to the appropriate blank. Remember to fill in a response option (1, 2, 3, 4, 5) for every statement.

1. _____	2. _____	3. _____	4. _____	5. _____
6. _____	7. _____	8. _____	9. _____	10. _____
11. _____	12. _____	13. _____	14. _____	15. _____
16. _____	17. _____	18. _____	19. _____	20. _____
21. _____	22. _____	23. _____	24. _____	25. _____
26. _____	27. _____	28. _____	29. _____	30. _____

If the name of the person who asked you to complete the Student LPI-Observer is not written below or on the first page, please add it yourself:_____

FURTHER INSTRUCTIONS

You should have received instructions to:

☐ Bring this page with you to the class (seminar or workshop) or

☐ Return this form to:

_____

_____

_____

_____

For more information on The Student LPI and *The Student Leadership Challenge,* including books, workbooks, and other learning materials, go to www.studentleadershipchallenge.com.

_____

To contact Jossey-Bass directly call our Customer Care Department within the U.S. at 800–956–7739, outside the U.S. at 317–572–3986, or fax 317–572–4002.

ISBN10: 0–7879–8030–7, ISBN13: 978–07879–8030–6
Printed in the United States of America
Printing 20 19 18 17 16 15 14 13 12

ISBN 978-0-7879-8030-6

JAMES M. KOUZES | BARRY Z. POSNER

Student Leadership Practices Inventory

SECOND EDITION

[OBSERVER]

Student Leadership Practices Inventory

by James M. Kouzes | Barry Z. Posner

[OBSERVER]

INSTRUCTIONS

On the next two pages are thirty statements describing various leadership behaviors. Please read each statement carefully. Then **rate the person who asked you to complete this form** about *how frequently* he or she engages in the behavior described. *This is not a test* (there are no right or wrong answers).

Consider each statement in the context of a student organization with which the person you are describing is most involved with or with which you have had the greatest opportunity to observe him or her. This organization could be a club, team, chapter, group, unit, hall, program, project, and the like. Maintain a *consistent* organizational perspective as you respond to each statement. The rating scale provides five choices:

1   If this person RARELY or SELDOM does what is described

2   If this person does what is described ONCE IN A WHILE

3   If this person SOMETIMES does what is described

4   If this person OFTEN does what is described

5   If this person VERY FREQUENTLY or ALMOST ALWAYS does what is described

- Be realistic about the extent to which this person actually engages in the behavior.
- Be as honest and accurate as you can be.
- *Do not* answer in terms of how you would like this person to behave or in terms of how you or someone else might think the person should behave.
- *Do* answer in terms of how this person typically engages on most days, on most projects, with most people.
- Be thoughtful about your responses; giving all fives or all threes or all ones is most likely not an accurate description. Most people will do some things more or less often than they do other things.
- If you feel a statement does not apply, it's probably because you don't observe this person engaging in the behavior; and, in that case, simply circle the number 1.
- Please respond to every statement.

For each statement, decide on a response and then circle the corresponding number to the right of the statement. For example, the first statement is "This person sets a personal example of what he or she expects from other people." If you believe the person does this *once in a while*, circle the number 2. If you believe the person sets a personal example of what he or she expects from others fairly *often*, circle the number 4. Select and circle only one option (response number) for each statement.

When you have responded to all thirty statements, please turn to the response sheet on the back page and transfer your responses as instructed.

Name of the individual whom you are thinking about in responding to these statements: _____

How frequently does this person *typically* engage in the following behaviors and actions? *Circle* the number to the right of each statement, using the scale below, that best applies.

1	2	3	4	5
RARELY OR SELDOM	ONCE IN A WHILE	SOMETIMES	OFTEN	VERY FREQUENTLY

1.	Sets a personal example of what he or she expects from other people.	1 2 3 4 5
2.	Looks ahead and communicates about what he or she believes will affect us in the future.	1 2 3 4 5
3.	Looks for ways to develop and challenge people's skills and abilities.	1 2 3 4 5
4.	Fosters cooperative rather than competitive relationships among people he or she works with.	1 2 3 4 5
5.	Praises people for a job well done.	1 2 3 4 5
6.	Spends time making sure that people behave consistently with the principles and standards that have been agreed upon.	1 2 3 4 5
7.	Describes to others in the organization what we should be capable of accomplishing.	1 2 3 4 5
8.	Looks for ways that others can try out new ideas and methods.	1 2 3 4 5
9.	Actively listens to diverse points of view.	1 2 3 4 5
10.	Encourages others as they work on activities and programs.	1 2 3 4 5
11.	Follows through on the promises and commitments he or she makes.	1 2 3 4 5
12.	Talks with others about a vision of how things could be even better in the future.	1 2 3 4 5
13.	Searches for innovative ways to improve what is being done.	1 2 3 4 5
14.	Treats others with dignity and respect.	1 2 3 4 5
15.	Expresses appreciation for the contributions that people make.	1 2 3 4 5
16.	Seeks to understand how his or her actions affect other people's performance.	1 2 3 4 5
17.	Talks with others about how their own interests can be met by working toward a common goal.	1 2 3 4 5
18.	When things do not go as he or she expected, asks, "What can we learn from this experience?"	1 2 3 4 5
19.	Supports the decisions that other people make on their own.	1 2 3 4 5
20.	Makes it a point to publicly recognize people who show commitment to shared values.	1 2 3 4 5
21.	Makes sure that people support the values that have been agreed upon.	1 2 3 4 5
22.	Is upbeat and positive when talking about what could be accomplished.	1 2 3 4 5
23.	Makes sure that big projects undertaken are broken down into smaller and doable parts.	1 2 3 4 5
24.	Gives others a great deal of freedom and choice in deciding how to do their work.	1 2 3 4 5
25.	Finds ways for people to celebrate accomplishments.	1 2 3 4 5
26.	Talks about his or her values and the principles that guide his or her actions.	1 2 3 4 5
27.	Speaks with passion about the higher purpose and meaning of what is being done.	1 2 3 4 5
28.	Takes initiative in experimenting with the way things can be done.	1 2 3 4 5
29.	Provides opportunities for others to take on leadership responsibilities.	1 2 3 4 5
30.	Makes sure that people are creatively recognized for their contributions.	1 2 3 4 5

TRANSFERRING THE RESPONSES

After you have responded to the thirty statements on the previous page, please transfer your responses to the blanks below. This will make it easier to record and score your responses.

Notice that the numbers of the statements are listed *horizontally* across the page. Make sure that the number you assigned to each statement is transferred to the appropriate blank. Remember to fill in a response option (1, 2, 3, 4, 5) for every statement.

1. _____	2. _____	3. _____	4. _____	5. _____
6. _____	7. _____	8. _____	9. _____	10. _____
11. _____	12. _____	13. _____	14. _____	15. _____
16. _____	17. _____	18. _____	19. _____	20. _____
21. _____	22. _____	23. _____	24. _____	25. _____
26. _____	27. _____	28. _____	29. _____	30. _____

If the name of the person who asked you to complete the Student LPI-Observer is not written below or on the first page, please add it yourself: _____

FURTHER INSTRUCTIONS

You should have received instructions to:

☐ Bring this page with you to the class (seminar or workshop) or

☐ Return this form to:

_____

_____

_____

_____

For more information on The Student LPI and *The Student Leadership Challenge*, including books, workbooks, and other learning materials, go to www.studentleadershipchallenge.com.

Copyright © 2013 by James M. Kouzes and Barry Z. Posner. All rights reserved.
Published by Jossey-Bass
A Wiley Imprint
1 Montgomery, Suite 1200, San Francisco, CA 94104 www.jossey-bass.com/highereducation

To contact Jossey-Bass directly call our Customer Care Department within the U.S. at 800–956–7739, outside the U.S. at 317–572–3986, or fax 317–572–4002.

ISBN10: 0–7879–8030–7, ISBN13: 978–07879–8030–6
Printed in the United States of America
Printing 20 19 18 17 16 15 14 13 12

ISBN 978-0-7879-8030-6

JAMES M. KOUZES | BARRY Z. POSNER

STUDENT
LPI

Student Leadership Practices Inventory

SECOND EDITION

[SELF]

Student Leadership Practices Inventory

by James M. Kouzes | Barry Z. Posner

[SELF]

INSTRUCTIONS

On the next two pages are thirty statements describing various leadership behaviors. Please read each statement carefully. Then rate yourself in terms of *how frequently* you engage in the behavior described. *This is not a test* (there are no right or wrong answers).

The rating scale provides five choices. Using the scale below, ask yourself:

"How frequently do I engage in the behavior described?"

1 If you RARELY or SELDOM do what is described

2 If you do what is described ONCE IN A WHILE

3 If you SOMETIMES do what is described

4 If you OFTEN do what is described

5 If you VERY FREQUENTLY or ALMOST ALWAYS do what is described

- Be realistic about the extent to which you actually engage in the behavior.
- Be as honest and accurate as you can be.
- *Do not* answer in terms of how you would like to behave or in terms of how you or someone else might think you should behave.

- *Do* answer in terms of how you typically engage on most days, on most projects, with most people.
- Be thoughtful about your responses; giving yourself all fives or all threes or all ones is most likely not an accurate description of your behavior. Most people will do some things more or less often than they do other things.
- If you feel a statement does not apply to you, it's probably because you don't frequently engage in the behavior; and, in that case, simply circle the number 1.
- Please respond to every statement.

For each statement, decide on a response and then circle the corresponding number to the right of the statement. For example, the first statement is "I set a personal example of what I expect from other people." If you believe you do this *once in a while*, then circle the number 2. If you believe you set a personal example of what you expect from others fairly *often*, circle the number 4. Select and circle only one option (response number) for each statement.

When you have responded to all thirty statements, please turn to the response sheet on the back page and transfer your responses as instructed.

Your Name:_____

How frequently do you *typically* engage in the following behaviors and actions? *Circle* the number to the right of each statement, using the scale below, that best applies.

1	2	3	4	5
RARELY OR SELDOM	ONCE IN A WHILE	SOMETIMES	OFTEN	VERY FREQUENTLY

1.	I set a personal example of what I expect from other people.	1	2	3	4	5
2.	I look ahead and communicate about what I believe will affect us in the future.	1	2	3	4	5
3.	I look for ways to develop and challenge my skills and abilities.	1	2	3	4	5
4.	I foster cooperative rather than competitive relationships among people I work with.	1	2	3	4	5
5.	I praise people for a job well done.	1	2	3	4	5
6.	I spend time making sure that people behave consistently with the principles and standards we have agreed upon.	1	2	3	4	5
7.	I describe to others in our organization what we should be capable of accomplishing.	1	2	3	4	5
8.	I look for ways that others can try out new ideas and methods.	1	2	3	4	5
9.	I actively listen to diverse points of view.	1	2	3	4	5
10.	I encourage others as they work on activities and programs in our organization.	1	2	3	4	5
11.	I follow through on the promises and commitments I make.	1	2	3	4	5
12.	I talk with others about a vision of how things could be even better in the future.	1	2	3	4	5
13.	I search for innovative ways to improve what we are doing.	1	2	3	4	5
14.	I treat others with dignity and respect.	1	2	3	4	5
15.	I express appreciation for the contributions that people make.	1	2	3	4	5
16.	I seek to understand how my actions affect other people's performance.	1	2	3	4	5
17.	I talk with others about how their own interests can be met by working toward a common goal.	1	2	3	4	5
18.	When things do not go as we expected, I ask, "What can we learn from this experience?"	1	2	3	4	5
19.	I support the decisions that other people make on their own.	1	2	3	4	5
20.	I make it a point to publicly recognize people who show commitment to shared values.	1	2	3	4	5
21.	I make sure that people support the values we have agreed upon.	1	2	3	4	5
22.	I am upbeat and positive when talking about what we can accomplish.	1	2	3	4	5
23.	I make sure that big projects we undertake are broken down into smaller and doable parts.	1	2	3	4	5
24.	I give others a great deal of freedom and choice in deciding how to do their work.	1	2	3	4	5
25.	I find ways for us to celebrate accomplishments.	1	2	3	4	5
26.	I talk about my values and the principles that guide my actions.	1	2	3	4	5
27.	I speak with passion about the higher purpose and meaning of what we are doing.	1	2	3	4	5
28.	I take initiative in experimenting with the way things can be done.	1	2	3	4	5
29.	I provide opportunities for others to take on leadership responsibilities.	1	2	3	4	5
30.	I make sure that people are creatively recognized for their contributions.	1	2	3	4	5

TRANSFERRING THE RESPONSES

After you have responded to the thirty statements on the previous page, please transfer your responses to the blanks below. This will make it easier to record and score your responses.

Notice that the numbers of the statements are listed *horizontally* across the page. Make sure that the number you assigned to each statement is transferred to the appropriate blank. Remember to fill in a response option (1, 2, 3, 4, 5) for every statement.

1. _____	2. _____	3. _____	4. _____	5. _____
6. _____	7. _____	8. _____	9. _____	10. _____
11. _____	12. _____	13. _____	14. _____	15. _____
16. _____	17. _____	18. _____	19. _____	20. _____
21. _____	22. _____	23. _____	24. _____	25. _____
26. _____	27. _____	28. _____	29. _____	30. _____

FURTHER INSTRUCTIONS

Please write your name here: _____

You should have received instructions to:

☐ Bring this page with you to the class (seminar or workshop) or

☐ Return this form to:

_____

_____

_____

If you are interested in feedback from other people, ask them to complete the Student LPI-Observer. This form provides perspectives on your leadership behaviors as perceived by other people. You can find information for hand-entering Observer scores to analyze your results at www.studentleadershipchallenge.com under Assessments.

For more information on The Student LPI and *The Student Leadership Challenge*, including books, workbooks, and other learning materials, go to www.studentleadershipchallenge.com.

Copyright © 2013 by James M. Kouzes and Barry Z. Posner. All rights reserved.
Published by Jossey-Bass
A Wiley Imprint
1 Montgomery, Suite 1200, San Francisco, CA 94104 www.jossey-bass.com/highereducation

To contact Jossey-Bass directly call our Customer Care Department within the U.S. at 800–956–7739, outside the U.S. at 317–572–3986, or fax 317–572–4002.

ISBN10: 0–7879–8020–X, ISBN13: 978–07879–8020–7
Printed in the United States of America
Printing 20 19 18 17 16 15 14 13

ISBN 978-0-7879-8020-7

THE STUDENT LEADERSHIP CHALLENGE

Student Workbook and Personal Leadership Journal

JB JOSSEY-BASS™
A Wiley Brand

THE STUDENT LEADERSHIP CHALLENGE

Student Workbook and Personal Leadership Journal

James Kouzes and Barry Posner

With Beth High and Gary M. Morgan

WILEY

Published by Jossey-Bass
A Wiley Imprint
One Montgomery Street, Suite 1200, San Francisco, CA 94104-4594—www.josseybass.com

Jossey-Bass books and products are available through most bookstores. To contact Jossey-Bass directly call our Customer Care Department within the U.S. at 800-956-7739, outside the U.S. at 317-572-3986, or fax 317-572-4002.

Wiley publishes in a variety of print and electronic formats and by print-on-demand. Some material included with standard print versions of this book may not be included in e-books or in print-on-demand. If this book refers to media such as a CD or DVD that is not included in the version you purchased, you may download this material at http://booksupport.wiley.com. For more information about Wiley products, visit www.wiley.com.

ISBN: 978-1-118-39009-2 (paper)
ISBN: 978-1-118-59967-9 (ebk.)
ISBN: 978-1-118-59999-0 (ebk.)
ISBN: 978-1-118-60029-0 (ebk.)

Printed in the United States of America
FIRST EDITION

PB Printing   10 9 8 7 6 5 4 3 2 1

CONTENTS

THE
STUDENT
LEADERSHIP
CHALLENGE

Student Workbook
and Personal Leadership
Journal

Welcome to The Student Leadership Challenge

In today's world, there are countless opportunities to make a difference. More than ever before, there is a need for people of all ages, from all backgrounds, with all types of life experiences, to seize the opportunities that can lead to great success. More than ever before, there is a need for leaders to inspire people to dream, to participate, and to persevere.

The Student Leadership Challenge offers everyone the chance to do just that: to take the initiative and make a difference. This challenge is about how student leaders mobilize others to want to make extraordinary things happen in their organizations. It's about the practices leaders use to transform values into actions, visions into realities, obstacles into innovations, separateness into solidarity, and risks into rewards. It's about how students can create a climate in which people turn challenging opportunities into remarkable successes.

ABOUT THE STUDENT LEADERSHIP CHALLENGE

The foundation of this approach is The Five Practices of Exemplary Leadership model. The model began with a research project in 1983 that asked people, "What did you do when you were at your 'personal best' in leading others?"

Three decades later, The Five Practices of Exemplary Leadership model continues to prove its effectiveness as a clear, evidence-based path to achieving the extraordinary—for individuals, groups, organizations, and communities. It turns the abstract concept of leadership into easy-to-grasp practices and behaviors that can be taught to anyone willing to step up and accept the challenge to lead.

The evidence behind The Student Leadership Challenge supports the core philosophy that leadership is everyone's business. In *The Student Leadership Challenge,* actual case examples of young people who demonstrate each leadership practice and specific recommendations on what people can do to make each practice their own and continue their development as a leader are provided.

HOW TO USE THE STUDENT WORKBOOK

The student leaders we've worked with and learned from have asked us many questions about developing their leadership capabilities. In this *Student Workbook,* we offer a pathway for you to explore what the thirty leadership behaviors that make up The Five Practices of Exemplary Leadership are all about, offer opportunities for you to get some practice engaging with them, and help you define your ongoing leadership development journey.

Throughout the workbook, we often refer to leaders of groups and organizations: these leaders are the students we have studied—not just students in leadership positions, but students just like you who have taken the challenge and worked with others to make extraordinary things happen in groups and organizations they are part of. We use the terms *groups* and *organizations* to encompass as many examples as possible. You do not need to be part of any official organization for The Student Leadership Challenge to be relevant and useful. The concepts, ideas, and action are equally applicable for groups, committees, formal organizations, and even class projects.

Module 1 introduces our point of view about leadership, reviews the origins of The Student Leadership Challenge, and provides an activity to help you identify the leader within you. It also provides an overview of The Five Practices of Exemplary Leadership model.

Module 2 is about the Student Leadership Practices Inventory (LPI) and provides guidance for getting the most out of your Student LPI report. This module includes an overview of the instrument, help with interpreting the report it generates, and suggested ways to use the results to support your ongoing leadership development journey.

Modules 3 through 7 explore each of The Five Practices in depth. We have designed each of those modules to describe one leadership practice and explain the two essential action components of that practice that student leaders employ to make extraordinary things happen. Collectively, we refer to these actions as the Ten Commitments of Leadership (Figure I.1).

Figure I.1 The Five Practices and Ten Commitments of Exemplary Leadership

Model the Way	1. Clarify values by finding your voice and affirming shared values. 2. Set the example by aligning actions with shared values.
Inspire a Shared Vision	3. Envision the future by imagining exciting and ennobling possibilities. 4. Enlist others in a common vision by appealing to shared aspirations.
Challenge the Process	5. Search for opportunities by seizing the initiative and looking outward for innovative ways to improve. 6. Experiment and take risks by constantly generating small wins and learning from experience.
Enable Others to Act	7. Foster collaboration by building trust and facilitating relationships. 8. Strengthen others by increasing self-determination and developing competence.
Encourage the Heart	9. Recognize contributions by showing appreciation for individual excellence. 10. Celebrate the values and victories by creating a spirit of community.

Source: The Leadership Challenge, 5th edition, by James M. Kouzes and Barry Z. Posner. San Francisco: Jossey-Bass, 2012.

Figure I.2 The Five Practices Model Structure

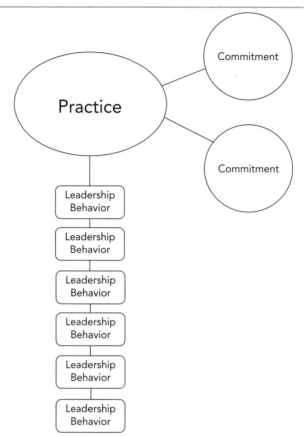

Each module also contains a list of the six leadership behaviors associated with that practice from the Student LPI and ways you can take action to demonstrate the behaviors more frequently. The relationship between The Five Practices, the Ten Commitments, and the thirty behaviors is diagrammed in Figure I.2.

Along the way, we suggest steps to take, sometimes alone and sometimes with others, to build your skills in becoming a better leader. Whether the focus is your own learning or the development of others in your group, you can take immediate action on every one of the recommendations. They require little or no budget and don't require you to have any elaborate or extensive discussions, build consensus among peers, or be preapproved: they just require your personal commitment and discipline.

Module 8, Your Personal Leadership Journal, is designed to support you as you face the challenge of practicing exemplary leadership each day. It walks you through the most effective form of practice: taking deliberate action, reflecting on and learning from the outcome, and taking action again.

It's been said that the education and development of people is the lever to change the world, and we believe this is especially true for you as an emerging leader. In these extraordinary times, there is no shortage of challenging opportunities, and the challenges seem to be increasing in number and complexity. But remember that all generations confront their own serious threats and receive their own favorable circumstances. The abundance of challenges is not the issue: it's how you respond to them that matters. Through your responses, you have the potential to seriously worsen or profoundly improve the world in which you live, study, play, and work.

By improving your abilities to lead, you will be better able to effect the kinds of positive changes that are needed. You will be better able to make a difference in the quality of your life and the lives of others. We know from our research that you have the capacity to learn to lead and the capacity to make extraordinary things happen. We believe in you, and we thank you for challenging yourself to liberate and develop the leader within.

James M. Kouzes

Barry Z. Posner

MODULE 1
Introduction

CORE PHILOSOPHY OF THE STUDENT LEADERSHIP CHALLENGE

We have found that students struggle with thinking of themselves as leaders. What do you think? Are you are a leader? We believe the answer is a resounding "Yes!" Think back to one of your own personal-best leadership experiences. We believe you will see that you already know what it takes to lead others. But knowing is not enough; to become the best leader you can be, you need to practice deliberately and often. Here are eight key concepts that The Leadership Challenge research reveals are true about leadership.

1. Leadership Is Everyone's Business

Being an effective leader is not limited to a few charismatic young people. It is not a gene or an inheritance. The theory that only a select few can lead others to greatness is just plain wrong. Leadership is not a position or rank, but a responsibility people choose to embrace throughout their lives.

One question that frequently comes up from students is: "If everyone is a leader, then how can everyone be a leader at once? Shouldn't there be just one leader?" We believe that everyone can be a leader, but that people will make a choice about when they step up to lead based on the values they hold. Commonly there is only one positional leader at a time, but this doesn't prevent others from taking a leadership role within their area of influence. For example, you might not be the president of your fraternity or sorority, but you certainly can choose to demonstrate leadership behaviors on the committees and groups that are part of that larger organization. You may not be an officer in student government or the captain of a team, but you can take the initiative to start a campaign that will improve the quality of student life. There are also many facets of your life. Your position as head of an organization is not the only place where you can act as a leader. You have opportunities to lead in many different situations: in your home, your school, and your community.

2. Leadership Is Learned

Leadership is a process that ordinary people use when they are bringing out the best in themselves and others. It is an identifiable set of skills and abilities that is available to everyone.

3. Leadership Is a Relationship

At the heart of leadership is the ability to connect with others, understand their hopes and dreams, and engage them in pulling together for a shared dream of the future. Leaders understand that every relationship contributes to their ability to be successful.

4. Leadership Development Is Self-Development

Engineers have computers, painters have brushes and paints, musicians have instruments. Leaders have only themselves: that is their instrument. Committing to liberating the leader within is a personal commitment. The journey begins with an exploration of who you are from the inside out.

5. Learning to Lead Is an Ongoing Process

Learning to lead is a journey, not a single event or destination. You may occupy many leadership roles throughout your life. Each will deepen your understanding of what it takes to engage others and what it takes to inspire others to make extraordinary things happen with people in your life. The context in which you lead will change, and with each change comes deeper learning. The best leaders are the best learners.

6. Leadership Requires Deliberate Practice

Excellence in anything—whether it's music, sports, or academics—requires deliberate practice. Leadership is no exception. You will need to devote time every day to becoming the best leader you can be.

7. Leadership Is an Aspiration and a Choice

Leaders have countless chances to make a difference. If a person wants to lead others and is willing to do the work, he or she can lead. It is a deeply personal choice and a lifetime commitment.

8. Leadership Makes a Difference

All leadership is based on one fundamental assumption: that *you* matter. We know from The Leadership Challenge research that every leader can make a profound difference in the lives of others. To do that, you have to believe in yourself and in your capacity to have a positive influence on others. And we also know that to those who are following you, *you* are the most important leader to them at that moment. It's not some other leader. It's you. You are the person whom group members will most likely go to for examples of how to tackle challenging goals, respond to difficult situations, handle crises, or deal with setbacks. We say a little more about this in the final section of this workbook "Onward!"

A Definition of Leadership

Leadership is the art of mobilizing others to want to struggle for shared aspirations.

In the academic literature, there are hundreds of different definitions of leadership. The research that resulted in The Five Practices of Exemplary Leadership led to the following definition of leadership, which incorporates what the evidence revealed:

What words stand out to you in this definition?

ACTIVITY 1.1

Your Personal-Best Leadership Experience

The research to discover what exemplary leaders do when they are at their personal best began by collecting thousands of stories from ordinary people—from students to executives in all types of organizations around the globe—about the experiences they recalled when asked to think of a peak leadership experience, that is, what they did when they were at their personal best as a leader. The collection effort continues, and the stories continue to offer compelling examples of what leaders do when making extraordinary things happen. As you begin to explore *The Student Leadership Challenge* and The Five Practices of Exemplary Leadership, we ask you to respond to some of the same questions asked of those involved in the original research. It's called the *personal-best leadership experience,* and we believe it will provide you with an inspiring view of the leader within you.

Begin by thinking about a time when you performed at your very best as a leader. A personal-best experience is an event (or a series of events) that you believe to be your individual standard of excellence. It's your own record-setting performance—a time when you achieved significant success while working with others. It is something against which you can measure yourself to determine whether you are performing as a leader at levels you know to be possible.

Your personal-best experience may have happened when you had no official authority but chose to play a leadership role within a group, organization, class project, or even a family situation. Focus on one specific experience.

Step 1

On a separate sheet of paper, describe this leadership experience by answering the following questions:

* When did it happen? How long did it last?
* What was your role? Who else was involved?

- What feelings did you have prior to and during the experience?
- Did you initiate the experience? If someone else initiated it, how did you emerge as the leader?
- What were the results of the experience?

Step 2

With relation to this experience, on a separate sheet of paper, list the actions you took as a leader that made a difference, and answer the following questions:

- What actions did you take?
- How did you get others to go beyond the ordinary levels of performance?
- What did you do to demonstrate your own commitment to the project or undertaking?
- What did you do to make sure everyone understood the purpose or goal?
- What did you or others do to overcome any major challenges or setbacks?
- What did you do to engage others and get them to participate fully?
- Based on what you did or said, what other extraordinary actions did your team or group members take?
- Summarize what you consider to be the five to seven most important actions you took as a leader who made a difference.

Step 3

Review the responses from the questions in steps 1 and 2. What three to five major lessons did you learn about leadership from this experience? (These are lessons you might share as advice to others about them being or becoming a great leader.) Write them here:

Lesson 1:

Lesson 2:

Lesson 3:

Lesson 4:

Lesson 5:

Step 4

From the lessons you identified in step 3:

- What single piece of advice would you give to another individual on how to make extraordinary things happen in their organization based on your experience?

Step 5

Follow your instructor's directions on how to share your story with others (using the notes you took here). Hearing other personal-best experiences will deepen your perspective on the limitless opportunities for demonstrating excellence in leadership. As you listen to others' stories, look for common qualities you see in the stories—for example, excellent communication, focus, or doing more than what was expected.

THE FIVE PRACTICES OF EXEMPLARY LEADERSHIP MODEL

This workbook has its origins in a research project begun more than thirty years ago. To learn what people did when they were at their personal best in leading others, we interviewed hundreds of people using the same types of questions you used to reflect on your personal-best leadership experience. The starting assumption was that asking regular people to describe extraordinary leadership experiences would reveal patterns of success. We believed we didn't need to interview and survey star performers or top executives in excellent companies to discover best practices. The majority of leaders in the world are not in senior positions, don't make the covers of magazines, and aren't in the daily news. To determine exemplary leadership practices, you have to ask leaders at all levels, in all endeavors, and of all ages.

Analyzing thousands of students' responses to the personal-best leadership experience—the kinds of responses you've heard from your colleagues—showed that despite differences in culture, gender, or age these personal-best stories revealed similar patterns of behavior. No matter where a personal-best experience took place—whether it was in a classroom, a student club or organization, a sports team, a community service project, a part-time job, a religious or spiritual organization, or on a school field trip—when leaders were at their personal best, there were then, and are today, five core leadership practices common to all these examples: Model the Way, Inspire a Shared Vision, Challenge the Process, Enable Others to Act, and Encourage the Heart.

Model the Way: Clarify Values and Set the Example

Leaders clarify values by finding their voice and affirming shared values, and they set the example by aligning actions with shared values.

The most important personal quality people look for and admire in a leader is personal credibility. Credibility is the foundation of leadership. If people don't believe in the messenger, they won't believe the message.

Leaders clarify values and establish guiding principles concerning the way people (fellow students, student groups, teachers, and advisors) should be treated and the way goals should be pursued. They create standards of excellence and then set an example for others to follow.

Titles may be granted, but leadership is earned. Leaders earn credibility by putting their values into action and living by the same standards and principles they expect of others. Leaders not only talk about the way things should be done; they show the way they should be done.

Figure 1.1 **The Five Practices of Exemplary Leadership**

Inspire a Shared Vision: Envision the Future and Enlist Others

Leaders envision the future by imagining exciting and ennobling possibilities, and they enlist others in a common vision by appealing to shared aspirations.

Leaders are driven by their clear image of possibility and what their organization could become. They passionately believe that they can make a difference. They envision the future, creating an ideal and unique image of what the group, team, or organization can be. Leaders enlist others in their dreams. They breathe life into their visions and get people to see exciting possibilities for the future.

Challenge the Process: Search for Opportunities and Experiment and Take Risks

Leaders search for opportunities by seizing the initiative and looking outward for innovative ways to improve. They experiment and take risks by constantly generating small wins and learning from experience.

Leaders are pioneers—they are willing to step out into the unknown. The work of leaders is change, and the status quo is unacceptable to them. They search for opportunities to innovate, grow, and improve. In doing so, they experiment and take risks. Because leaders know that risk taking involves mistakes and failures, they accept the inevitable disappointments as learning opportunities. Leaders constantly ask, "What can we learn when things don't go as planned?"

Enable Others to Act: Foster Collaboration and Strengthen Others

Leaders foster collaboration by building trust and facilitating relationships. They strengthen others by enhancing self-determination and developing competence.

Leaders know they can't do it alone. Leadership involves building relationships and is a group effort. Leaders foster collaboration and create spirited groups. They actively involve others. Leaders understand that they have a responsibility to bring others along.

Collaboration is the master skill that enables groups, partnerships, and other alliances to function effectively. The work of leaders is making people feel strong, capable, informed, and connected.

Encourage the Heart: Recognize Contributions and Celebrate the Values and Victories

Leaders recognize contributions by showing appreciation for individual excellence. They celebrate the values and victories by creating a spirit of community.

Accomplishing extraordinary things in groups and organizations is hard work. The climb to the top is arduous and long; people can become exhausted, frustrated, and disenchanted. They're often tempted to give up. Genuine acts of caring uplift the spirit and draw people forward. To keep hope and determination alive, leaders recognize the contributions that individuals make. In every winning team, the members need to share in the rewards of their efforts, so leaders celebrate accomplishments. They make people feel like heroes.

Embedded within these Five Practices are thirty essential leadership behaviors that are the basis for The Student Leadership Practices Inventory (Student LPI) and are described in the next module. To get the most out of your leadership development opportunity, you should complete the Student LPI. The instrument provides you with a way to measure how frequently you are currently engaging in each of the thirty behaviors.

MODULE 2
Your Student LPI

WHAT IS THE STUDENT LPI?

The Student Leadership Practices Inventory is a comprehensive leadership development tool designed to help you measure your leadership behaviors and enable you to take action to improve your effectiveness as a leader. The assessment is made up of the Student LPI Self Assessment (which you complete) and the Student LPI Observer (anonymously completed by others chosen by either you or the person administrating your Student LPI), making it a comprehensive look at the frequency with which you engage in The Five Practices of Exemplary Leadership.

Student LPI Self Assessment

This thirty-item self-assessment measures the frequency of specific leadership behaviors on a five-point scale. It takes approximately ten to fifteen minutes to complete.

Student LPI Observer Assessment

This assessment provides 360-degree feedback on the frequency of specific leadership behaviors on a five-point frequency scale. Completed by individuals selected by you or the person administrating your assessment, it takes approximately ten to fifteen minutes to complete.

While this assessment provides for self-measurement, the greater value in the assessment is using the Student LPI Observer feature. This unique measurement tool collects valuable feedback for you from teachers, coaches, student advisors, teammates, fellow club members, coworkers, or others who have direct experience in observing you in a leadership role or any leadership capacity.

Who Is the Student LPI Designed For?

Even if you don't identify yourself as a leader, the research behind The Student Leadership Challenge indicates that everyone has the potential to lead. The Student LPI tool is designed for students with little to no formal professional experience, and it is appropriate in high school and college classrooms, student government, campus clubs, fraternities, sororities, first-year-experience programs, community service and service-learning organizations, athletic teams, and youth organizations. If you are looking to enhance your leadership role in your school or community, you will benefit from using the Student LPI to learn how you use The Five Practices framework and consider how you could make more use of the model as you encounter real-life challenges and opportunities.

How Many Observers Should I Have, and Whom Should I Choose?

We recommend at least five observers, which may mean asking eight or more people in case there are some who do not complete the assessment. Choose teachers, coaches, student advisors, teammates, fellow club members, coworkers, or others who have direct experience in observing you in a leadership role or any leadership capacity. It's a great idea to send an e-mail in advance requesting that they do this, reminding them that their feedback is anonymous, and articulating what you hope to get out of the experience.

UNDERSTANDING YOUR STUDENT LPI RESULTS

It is important to understand your results and think about them appropriately. The Student LPI is not about attitudes or intentions but about actual behaviors. The assessment contains thirty behavior-based statements. Each one asks you about a specific leadership behavior and the extent to which you engage in that behavior.

The Student LPI uses a five-point scale to measure the frequency with which you demonstrate (Self) or others (Observers) observe you demonstrating the behavior.

Score	Meaning
1	You rarely or seldom engage in the behavior. For your observers, this score indicates they rarely or seldom see you engage in the behavior.
2	You engage in the behavior once in a while. For your observers, this score indicates they see you engage in the behavior once in a while.
3	You sometimes engage in the behavior. For your observers, this score indicates they see you engage in the behavior sometimes.
4	You engage in the behavior often. For your observers, this score indicates they see you engage in the behavior often.
5	You engage in the behavior very frequently or almost always. For your observers, this score indicates they see you engage in the behavior very frequently or almost always.

A common question is, "Why isn't there a designation of N/A or 'Does not apply'?" Because the response calls for a measure of frequency, a "does not apply" designation is not relevant. If you believe you are not in a position to demonstrate a behavior, perhaps you believe opportunities are available only in positions of leadership. The Student Leadership Challenge approach indicates that is not the case. When an observer wants to say "does not apply" because "I don't see this person doing this" or "I'm not in a position to know if the person does this," it is entirely appropriate for him or her to simply use response 1: the person seldom or rarely engages in this behavior from my vantage point. Certainly the goal is to select observers who have seen you in action and have data to draw on when responding to the instrument.

Each of the thirty behaviors from the Student LPI Self and Student LPI Observer instruments aligns with one of The Five Practices of Exemplary Leadership. Model the Way aligns to statements 1, 6, 11, 16, 21, and 26. These are the statements that relate to behaviors involved in Model the Way, such as clarifying values and setting an example. Statements 2, 7, 12, 17, 22, and 27 align with Inspire a Shared Vision, which involves envisioning the future and enlisting the support of others. Statements 3, 8, 13, 18, 23, and 28 align with Challenge the Process, which involves searching for opportunities, experimenting, and learning from mistakes. Enable Others to Act links to statements 4, 9, 14, 19, 24, and 29. This practice involves fostering collaboration and strengthening others. And Encourage the Heart pertains to statements 5, 10, 15, 20, 25, and 30, which involve recognizing contributions and celebrating values and victories.

The Student LPI provides feedback generated from you and others about how frequently you engage in these behaviors and actions that the research indicates are the practices and behaviors people demonstrate when they are leading effectively and making a difference.

How to Think about Your Student LPI Results

It's important to recognize that the Student LPI report is not a judgment of how well you do these practices, but a collection of observations about how often you do them and are seen doing them. Your opportunity is to explore the report in order to better understand yourself and find opportunities to increase the frequency with which you engage in the leadership behaviors. What behaviors can you do more often that could help you be more successful as a leader? How can you best demonstrate those behaviors? Many people have a tendency to be very hard on themselves and are quick to judge.

Keep in mind that this report is intended to be a development tool, not a test score; it is about frequency of observed behavior, not a judgment of your abilities. You might think of it as a snapshot in time, and like any other snapshot, there is some truth in it, but much more that is unclear or out of the picture. You've most likely seen a snapshot of yourself and thought "OMG, I look awful!" or, "Wow, I look great!" Remember that it's not the picture that matters; it's what you do as a result of seeing it.

We anticipate that most people will see significant changes in their Student LPI scores over time. As you learn new behaviors, experiment with different techniques, and hone specific skills, your skills are likely to increase in one or more practices. Of course, it's also possible for scores to fall over time as well. The Five Practices of Exemplary Leadership model affords you an easy-to-recall model to help you keep all thirty of these research-proved leadership behaviors in mind and in your daily leadership practice.

Another common response people have when receiving this feedback is to focus on the messenger, not the overall message. Instead of spending your time and energy trying to figure out who said what, work to understand the larger message from the feedback and take ownership of it. The responsibility to change lies with you and you alone.

Here are some questions that people commonly ask about their feedback:

What are the right answers?

There are no universal right answers when it comes to leadership. Still, the research indicates that the more frequently you are perceived as engaging in the behavior and actions identified in the Student LPI, the more likely it is that you will be an effective leader.

Should my perceptions be consistent with the ratings other people give me?

The general answer to this question is yes, although there may be understandable exceptions, which we discuss when we look at the actual data. People are generally more effective when their self-perceptions match the perceptions of them provided by other people.

Can I change my leadership behavior?

The answer to this question is categorically yes. Leadership is a skill like any other skill, which means that your motivation and dedication to improve, along with feedback, practice, and good coaching, can bring about improvements. However, remember that few people improve any skill dramatically overnight or in a single attempt.

USING YOUR STUDENT LPI FOR YOUR DEVELOPMENT AS A LEADER

The responsibility to change lies with you alone. The Student LPI provides a framework for you to develop routine practice opportunities. If you wanted to become good at a sport or accomplished at playing a certain instrument, you would spend time practicing. The same is true of leadership, and the Student LPI gives you the information you need to focus your practice. One option is to tie your individual report to the Personal Leadership Journal in Module 8 in this workbook. After you review your report, identify one of the practices and a specific behavior within it. Use that to start your plan and define what you will do to demonstrate that specific behavior soon.

Take any opportunity to connect with others to share your thoughts and intentions around your Student LPI results. You might schedule a regular conversation peer to peer, or perhaps you can identify a mentor. Sharing this information can help you effectively plan for your personal leadership development and be accountable for the actions you identify and commit to. The Personal Leadership Journal provides the format for reflecting on the action you took as well and the results it produced. Over time, you can track the results of the actions, record your thinking, and go back to the Student LPI for another target. This approach aligns solidly with the premise that leadership is a skill, and you get better at it with deliberate practice.

MODULE 3

Model the Way

PRACTICE SUMMARY

The first step a leader must take along the path to becoming an exemplary leader is inward. It's a step toward discovering personal values and beliefs. Leaders must find their voice, discover a set of principles that guide decisions and actions, and find a way to express a leadership philosophy in their own words, and not in someone else's.

Yet leaders don't speak just for themselves. They are often the voice for their team, their group, or their organization. Leadership is a dialogue, not a monologue. Therefore, they must reach out to others. They must understand and appreciate the values of their constituents and find a way to affirm shared values. Leaders forge unity. They don't force it. They give people reasons to care, not simply orders to follow.

Leaders stand up for their beliefs. They practice what they preach and show others by their actions that they live by the values they profess. They also ensure that others adhere to the values that have been agreed on. It is consistency between words and actions that build credibility.

This consistency of word and deed makes Model the Way the bedrock from which leaders can effectively engage in the other practices of exemplary leadership.

We highly recommend you read *The Student Leadership Challenge* book to deepen your understanding of The Five Practices of Exemplary Leadership model by reading about students who demonstrate the leadership behaviors embedded in the model. The stories in the book are intended to both inform and inspire you.

UNDERSTAND AND PRACTICE THE LEADERSHIP BEHAVIORS OF MODEL THE WAY

Leadership comes in all different forms and is mostly the model you provide for your peers in how you behave.

—NEIL KUCERA*

The following activities will help you explore and deepen your understanding of each of the six leadership behaviors that connect to Model the Way. Focus on one behavior at a time, and identify opportunities to demonstrate that behavior more often.

---

*All of the quotations displayed in *The Student Leadership Challenge Student Workbook* are from students in leadership classes and workshops around the world. In their own words, they talk about their personal-best leadership experiences, their most admired leaders, and the lessons they have learned about leadership. These same insights are likely to mirror your own experiences with leadership.

NOTE For each behavior, you will find two iterations of the statement that describes the behavior: (1) the statement as it appears in the Student LPI and (2) how the behavior is described in the student report that is generated from taking the Student LPI.*

MODEL
THE WAY

> "I talk about my values and the principles that guide my actions." (*Student LPI Report:* "Talks about values and principles.")

1.   List your five most important personal values. Describe what they mean to you; in other words, if you wrote one word or a short values phrase, write down the definition of what that means to you in action.

My Five Most Important Values and Their Definitions

A:

B:

C:

D:

E:

---

*This discussion does not present the behavior statements from the Student LPI in the order that they appear in the instrument. For developmental purposes, we decided that this was a better order to consider each of the essential behaviors associated with the leadership practice of Model the Way. This same consideration was applied in the other modules as well.

2. Compare your values to those of every group you are in. What is similar, and what is different? Are any of them different from any of your group's values that are difficult for you to live with? How will you reconcile the differences?

My Core Values	Values of the Groups I Am In	Match? Yes/No
A:		
B:		
C:		
D:		
E:		

Which do not match?

I will reconcile those values that don't match by:

3. Find three people with whom you feel you can talk about your values. Ask them if they knew these were things you stood for before you told them. If they reply yes, ask them how they knew. If they reply no, ask them what they perceive *is* important to you and why they believe that.

Name	They Know What I Value	Yes/How or No/Why Not?
A:		
B:		
C:		

Notes:

4. As you talk about your values, does your language or meaning for them change the more you describe them to others? If so, how? Write your refined definitions down as you get more clarity on what they mean to you.

I have refined my values, based on what I learned:

The biggest factor in motivating others to join the team was the fundamental personal belief in what I was doing.

—LEAH TOENISKOETTER

1. List three things you did in the past few weeks that you feel best exhibit who you are as a person, that is, what you value as important. What caused you or made you intentionally decide to do something that aligned with what you view as important to you?

> "I set a personal example of what I expect from other people." (*Student LPI report:* "Sets personal example.")

Three things I did in the past few weeks that were aligned with what I value:

A. My Actions

I know this action was aligned with my values because (What is it about your actions that demonstrates your values?):

B. My Actions

I know this action was aligned with my values because (What is it about your actions that actually demonstrate your values?):

C. My Actions

I know this action was aligned with my values because (What is it about your actions that actually demonstrates your values?):

2.   Considering the three items you listed, what can you do in addition to those? Write a sentence or two about the positive impact you have on a group or on others when your actions align with what you believe to be important. What do you notice about others' actions when your behavior is more aligned?

3.   Write a sentence or two about the impact you have on a group or on others when your actions *do not* align with what you believe to be important. Think about the actions you listed in question 1. Had you instead acted in ways that went against your values, what could have happened as a result?

4.   Ask any of the people with whom you've been talking about your values for examples of when they have seen you living out those values. Also ask for examples of times when they have heard you say or do things that are not in line with your values. Define an action you can take to continue or better live your values based on what you have learned.

Have seen me live out my values:

Value	Yes/How?	No/They Saw
A:		
B:		
C:		
D:		
E:		

5.   What are three recent occasions when you experienced someone in a group you belong to doing something different from what this person said he or she would do or committed to doing (he or she made a commitment but then did not follow through)? How did those actions affect you or others in the group?

A.

B.

C.

List three occasions where someone in the group did something different from what they committed to (do not list names, just the action):

A: Action

How did that person's actions affect me or others in the group?

B: Action

How did that person's actions affect me or others in the group?

C: Action

How did that person's actions affect me or others in the group?

6.   How does a group benefit from members who act in ways that support their values? Describe how a group can be affected when people (you or others) don't do what they say they will do.

MODEL THE WAY

> "I follow through on the promises and commitments I make." (*Student LPI Report:* "Follows through on promises.")

1.   What are the most recent three promises you made to someone else? Did you keep them (follow through on them)? If so, describe how. If not, describe why you didn't keep your promise. In either case, what impact did this have on your credibility with and relationship to others?

The last three promises I made:

Promise	Kept	Didn't Keep	Why/Impact
A			
B			
C			

2.   Make a list of commitments you have made to others in the past five days. Next to each item, write why you made that commitment. Next to that, write how much time (and any other relevant resources) you think the commitment will take (or did, if you fulfilled it).

The past five days I have committed to:

Commitment	Reason for Commitment	Time/Resources Required
A		
B		
C		
D		
E		

3.   When was the last time you made a commitment that you wish you had not? What was it? Did this commitment align with your goals? What about this experience detracted from your doing something more valuable? What else could you have done with this time that would have made a better impact?

Commitment I would take back:

Why:

A better use of my time would have been:

4.   Think about a recent time when you did not follow through on a commitment or promise. Write an action that you will take in the next forty-eight to seventy-two hours to work toward meeting that promise.

Commitment I did not follow through on:

To meet my commitment, in the next forty-eight to seventy-two hours I will:

5.   Think of the last time that you said no to a request, a group invitation, or something that involved an investment of your time. How did this make you feel? Did you feel emotions of missing out, or did you feel liberated by your decision?

I knew that my teammates, especially the younger ones, were looking up to me and would follow my behavior because that's what I did when I was in their shoes. I had to model the best behavior to set a standard for how to act.
—MATT STEELE

6.   Think about the commitments you have to others. Are you contributing value in each of the roles you take, or could someone else do as good a job or even better? If you considered remaining involved with the group in a lesser role, how might this affect your available time and your ability to execute?

"I seek to understand how my actions affect other people's performance." (Student LPI Report: "Seeks feedback about impact of actions.")

1. Describe the last time you asked someone for any type of feedback about something specific you did. What was the feedback for? What did the other person or people say to you? What did you do with that information? How did it feel?

Feedback requested:

Feedback was for:

The feedback I got was:

My reaction:

How I used this feedback:

2. What strong feelings, positive or negative, have you had in response to feedback that you have received? Why did you have that reaction? Was there anything in the feedback that you felt was accurate or productive even if you didn't respond positively to it?

Positive feelings:

Negative feelings:

Overall reaction (how I behaved in response to the feedback):

Useful lessons I took away from the feedback:

3.   Describe a time when you received feedback about something others thought you did really well. How have you or will you use that information to help repeat those or similar actions in the future?
Encouraging feedback I received:

To make this information useful, I will:

4.   In your next group meeting, ask three people for their thoughts about how you have related to your work with the group. Ask them to describe how they feel about your work. From the comments you receive, write down what you think the main themes are about how others described your work. Define a specific action step to take for one thing you want to repeat and one thing you want to work on and improve. As you take action on these two items, revisit your list of themes and select two more on which you can focus.
Person A:
   Comment:

Theme:

Action step—repeat:

Action step—improve:

Person B:

Comment:

Theme:

Action step—repeat:

Action step—improve:

Person C:

    Comment:

Theme:

Action step—repeat:

Action step—improve:

I learned that those who follow you are only as good as the model you present them with.

—JASON HEGLAND

MODEL
THE WAY

"I spend time making sure that people behave consistently with the principles and standards we have agreed upon." (*Student LPI Report:* "Aligns others with principles and standards.")

1.   List the values your group has established. Think about values as both your short-term goals that contribute to the definition of who your group is (e.g., your group might be service oriented, so are you doing things in the short term that are contributing to your group being of greater service to others as opposed to social activities?) and the group's values that your larger goals are based on (e.g., we are an academic-discipline-based group, so do we predominantly do things that promote greater knowledge in our subject matter or is more of our time and work focused on things that have nothing to do with intellectual and professional growth?).

Group values:

2.   From the list of values, name a time when you have talked about any of these and with whom:

I talked with _____ on _____ about the following values:

How do you both think you can live up to the values as individuals?

How do you both think the group lives up to the values?

What does it look like if the group doesn't live up to the values?

Together write an action you can share and take with the group to work toward living up to the values of the group:

How did this discussion go? Was it easy, hard, comfortable, or uncomfortable for you? What about for the other person? What did you learn about how you expressed your values to someone else?

3.   Without identifying specific people, make a list of behaviors you have seen group members exhibit in the past two weeks that represent the values of the group.

4.   Without identifying specific people, make a list of behaviors you have seen group members exhibit in the past two weeks that do not live up to the standards the group has set.

5.   Compare the items you listed in questions 3 and 4.

Think about the impact both lists have on the group and use that to help you lead a discussion. Discuss those in the next group gathering. Use what you have observed to suggest actions members of the group can take to continue to align their behavior to the group's goals and things they can do to better adhere to its standards.

MODEL
THE WAY

"I make sure that people support the values we have agreed upon." (*Student LPI Report:* "Makes sure people support common values.")

1. Define *consensus* for yourself. Ask five other people for their definition of *consensus*, and look for the similarities and differences in these definitions. Think about how these various definitions contribute to or detract from a group in reaching decisions.

Definitions of Consensus

Person A definition:

Person B definition:

Person C definition:

Person D definition:

Person E definition:

Pull out key words or phrases from all of the definitions and list below:

Similarities among the definitions:

Differences among the definitions:

2.   Think about both a time when you were with a group and reached consensus on something fairly easily and a time when the group had difficulty reaching consensus. How did each instance connect to the values of the group? When the situations didn't connect to the values of the group, share how they did not. What would you do to reach consensus and make certain that the work is aligned with the group's values?

3.   During one of the first few meetings, ask members of your group or team what they believe the core values of the group are. Make a list, and look for disparities and agreement. Have others describe where the group is or is not living out its values through decisions, changes they are considering, and other actions they take. This is an action you can revisit throughout the year, especially as new people come aboard.

When I asked others in the group what the group's *core* values were, they said:

A:

B:

C:

D:

E:

What is similar in these responses?

What is different in these responses?

To better align the group's values with our behaviors, I will work to:

To better align the group's values so they are clear to everyone, I will:

FURTHER ACTIONS TO IMPROVE IN MODEL THE WAY

A list of suggested actions follows that you can try out in order to improve in Model the Way. Some of the specific leadership behaviors in the Student LPI that are influenced by these actions are listed by number following each suggestion (see Appendix A for the complete list of Student LPI statements and behaviors).

1. At the beginning of each day, reflect about what you want to achieve for that day. Think in terms of what you know is important to you and what in your schedule contributes to that importance. You might ask yourself, "How do I want to show up as a leader today?" At the end of the day, reflect on what happened. What did you do as a leader that you are most proud of? Where were the opportunities that you missed that you could take advantage of another day? Can you do anything tomorrow about those opportunities? What other actions can you take tomorrow in which you can lead better? (1, 26)

2. If you are in a group and have a formal, defined leadership role, see how you can work directly with or shadow someone else in the group. In essence, trade places with that person and work on something together. Use this as an opportunity to get feedback from others as to what you are doing related to their work in the group. (6, 16)

3. Use a planner, smart phone, journal, note app, or some other resource regularly to write notes to yourself about the commitments and promises you are making to yourself and others. Write the dates on which you have committed to fulfilling them, and check regularly on your progress. (1, 11, 26)

4. Focus on the little things that your groups or the people you lead are doing. You can become easily engaged in the larger projects or tasks, but remember that it is the smaller details together that help others and the projects achieve success. Without micromanaging, look for places where you can make a difference. Think about how you use the smaller things that need attention to reinforce what you and the organization stand for. (1, 6, 16, 21, 26)

5. Keep track of how you spend your time. What is important to you and what you value often show up in how you spend your time and prioritize what you do every day and over the course of weeks and months. Look to see if you are investing large amounts of your time in things that are not that important to you or that you really don't value. The same might also be said about people and relationships. What can you do to adjust your schedule so that you are aligning your actions more with your values? (1, 6, 11, 21, 26)

6. If you are in an organized student group, visit other teams or groups at your school that are similar to and even different from yours that you know to be considered strong groups. Talk to their leaders, and ask what they are doing that could give you greater insight in leading. You don't have to be talking about doing the same things to learn and get feedback from how others lead and work. Learn what makes the other group so great. (16, 21, 26)

7. Study other leaders and organizations that you think live out their ideas and values as a group. These could be groups that you identified in action 6, or groups, organizations, or companies that are known to have strong values and demonstrate those values in their daily work. (1, 2, 16, 21)

ACTIVITIES TO LEARN ABOUT AND APPLY MODEL THE WAY

Activity 3.1

Values Spotlight

Overview

This activity helps you clarify or shine a light on your personal values. It also helps you understand the wide range of values people hold and the notion that there is no one right set of values. The activity can also be used to identify the values of a group.

Objectives

After completing this activity you will be able to:

*   Identify your top three personal values
*   Understand that there is not a single correct set of values
*   Understand that individuals have the right to hold any values they choose
*   Understand that individuals who don't hold the same values can effectively work together as a group and that the group will have its own set of values

Process

1. From the list of values provided at the end of the activity, pick your top ten values. Write them on an index card. You have two minutes to do this.

2. From your list of ten, choose your top three. Write each one on an index card. You have two minutes to do this.

3. Define each value on its index card in a sentence.

4. Answer the following questions:

   What did you notice about this activity?

   How do you feel knowing you may have different values than others in your group?

   Why do you think it's important to narrow down to just a few values?

Sample Values List

Achievement	Family time	Patience
Autonomy	Flexibility	Power
Beauty	Freedom	Productivity
Caring	Friendship	Profitability
Caution	Fun	Prosperity and wealth
Challenge	Growth	Quality
Communication	Happiness	Recognition
Competence	Harmony	Respect
Competition	Health	Responsibility
Courage	Honesty and integrity	Risk taking
Cooperation	Hope	Security
Creativity	Human relationships	Service to others
Curiosity	Humor	Simplicity
Customer focus	Independence	Speed
Decisiveness	Innovation	Spirituality and faith
Dependability	Individualism	Strength
Determination	Innovation	Success
Discipline	Intelligence	Task focus
Diversity	Involvement	Teamwork
Effectiveness	Learning	Trust
Empathy	Love and affection	Truth
Equality	Loyalty	Uniqueness
Falrness	Open-mindedness	Variety
Family	Organization	Winning
		Wisdom

Activity 3.2

Mark Your Calendars

Overview

This activity helps you examine the alignment of the values you claim and the way you spend your time. It's an alignment reality check. We recommend using this as a follow-up to Activity 3.1 where you identified your values. We also recommend you find a way to repeat this activity as an opportunity for personal reflection.

Objectives

After finishing this exercise, you will be able to:

- Account for the time you have spent in ways that align with your values
- Identify gaps in the alignment of your values and your actions
- Define ways to close those gaps

Process

1. Using the provided calendar, track everything you do for the amount of time defined. Include all activities, especially those you tend to overlook, like playing games on your favorite device, time watching movies or TV, or time on Facebook—all of it!
2. The next part of the activity begins after you have a chance to track your activities for the time period suggested by your facilitator.
3. Using the top three values index cards from Activity 3.1, review your activity calendars and think about how well your actions (and time spent) aligned with the values you said you hold.
4. Identify one thing you did that aligned well with one of your values.
5. Identify one thing you believe was not in alignment with your values.
6. Talk with a partner about what you found and how you could change one thing to be more in line with your values. Actively listen to what your partner has to say. We often get insight from others when we share our thinking and truly listen to the response.

Variation

You can also do this exercise as a planning exercise:

1. Using your top three values index cards, identify one thing you can do in the time frame defined that will align well with one of your values. *Example:* If "health" is one of your values, can you put a regular exercise into your planned time?
2. Talk with a partner about what you are planning and why. Then actively listen to what your partner has to say. We often get insight from others when we share our thinking and truly listen to the response.

Activity 3.3

Movie Activity: *Pay It Forward*

The Five Practices of Exemplary Leadership show up in many movies. This activity features selected movie clips that illustrate the use of Model the Way. Included is a brief synopsis of the film, a description of the clips that showcase the practice, and then a series of questions for you to answer or consider.

Movies are a great ways to spark your creative thinking about how The Five Practices show up in real life. While the clips listed here are clear examples of Model the Way, look for examples of any of the other practices or leadership behaviors.

Movie

2000. Director: Mimi Leder

Screenplay: Leslie Dixon

Distribution: Warner Bros. Pictures

Rated PG-13 for mature thematic elements including substances abuse and recovery, some sexual situations, language, and brief violence (no scenes for this activity include those elements).

This movie is based on the book of the same title written by Catherine Ryan Hyde about a boy who has an idea for an assignment in one of his classes to make the world a better place.

Synopsis

In the film, Trevor McKinney is a seventh grader. On the first day of the school year, his social studies teacher, Mr. Simonet, gives the class an assignment: each student in the class is to come up with an idea to change the world and put that idea into action. The lesson in this assignment is for the students to think about and figure out what the world means to them. Mr. Simonet hopes to teach his students that they will have a role to play in the world outside school.

Trevor's plan to change the world is based on an encounter he has with a homeless man. As a result of this encounter, Trevor decides he can change the world by "paying it forward." His plan is to do a good deed for three people, who then must do good deeds for three other people, and so on. The pyramid of good deeds grows as each person pays it forward.

Scene Descriptions

The following descriptions for four scenes in the film illustrate Model the Way. You can view these scenes as individual clips, stopping to discuss each in between, or as a collective sequence with discussion afterward.

Theme: Act of Generosity. Begins in chapter 1 of the DVD at approximately 0:01:50 to 0:04:11.

This clip shows a random act of kindness between two strangers. The scene sets the stage that leads to discovering Trevor's plan and also shows one example of the impact of his plan on others.

Theme: How About Possible. Begins in chapter 2 of the DVD at approximately 0:07:38 to chapter 3, 0:12:11.

Trevor's social studies teacher gives the class the assignment and leads a discussion about what the idea of changing the world could mean to his students. This scene depicts the students' resistance in their thinking that they can make a difference in the world around them.

Theme: That's the Idea. Begins in chapter 9 of the DVD at approximately 0:31:26 to chapter 10, 0:36:16.

This scene begins with an example of how Trevor's plan has begun to work. Trevor describes to the class his idea of paying it forward and how it works. The design of pay it forward requires each person to do something "big" that helps someone else in dealing with a challenging issue or meeting a need in his or her life.

Theme: Being Brave. Begins in chapter 31 of the DVD at approximately 1:46:59 to 1:50:46.

A newspaper reporter who has been following the movement of pay it forward discovers Trevor's role in it. Trevor records an interview with the reporter in which he describes what he thought had happened as a result of the class project. He describes his reasoning for why people have difficulty changing. The full power of pay it forward is realized in Trevor's description.

Leadership Lessons from *Pay It Forward*

Discussion Question for "Generosity"

1. What examples of Model the Way do you see in the opening scene, "Act of Generosity"?

Discussion Question for "Possible"

1. What do you notice about Mr. Simonet's answer to Trevor's question about what he did to change the world?

Discussion Question for "Idea"

1. What behaviors from Model the Way do you notice in the dialogue in the garage between Trevor's mother and Jerry, the homeless drug addict whom Trevor wants to help get back on his feet in his plan to do a good deed for three people, hoping they in turn will help three more and so on? As Trevor describes his plan to the class, what does he do that reflects the practice of Model the Way?

Discussion Question for "Brave"

1. In "Being Brave," what behaviors in the practice Model the Way do you hear about that were exhibited and held people back in paying it forward?

Discussion Question for All Scenes

1. In any of these scenes, what other practices or leadership behaviors did you notice?

CONNECT MODEL THE WAY TO MODULE 8: PERSONAL LEADERSHIP JOURNAL

The Personal Leadership Journal is available to help you shape your ongoing learning about each practice. There are three sections:

Section 1: Complete this section once you have had an opportunity to do a thorough review of your Student LPI report. You may be asked to complete this outside the classroom or formal workshop time, though that choice is up to your instructor. If you have not taken the Student LPI, complete this after you have a good understanding of Model the Way and the behaviors aligned with that practice.

Section 2: Complete this section after you have taken action. It will help guide you on to your next targeted action step.

Section 3: Use this section as a support tool for your ongoing and independent exploration of Model the Way.

MODULE 4

Inspire a Shared Vision

PRACTICE SUMMARY

The future holds little certainty. There are no guarantees or easy paths to any destinations, and circumstances can change in a heartbeat. Pioneering leaders rely on a compass and a dream and look forward to the future, holding in their minds visions and ideas of what can be. They have a sense of what is possible if everyone works together for a common purpose. They are positive about the future and passionately believe that people can make a difference.

But visions are insufficient to generate organized movement; others as well must see the exciting future possibilities. Leaders breathe life into visions. They communicate hopes and dreams so that others clearly understand and share them as their own and show others how their values and interests will be served by the long-term vision of the future.

As leaders start to imagine the possibilities, they must begin to create an ideal unique image of the future for the common good. They must visualize the details: what this image of the future looks, feels, and sounds like. They must paint a picture of it until it looks so real that they can articulate it with passion and conviction. Only then can they invite others to take part in creating this wonderful space.

Leaders are expressive, and they attract followers through their energy, optimism, and hope. With strong appeals and quiet persuasion, they develop enthusiastic supporters.

We highly recommend you read *The Student Leadership Challenge* book to deepen your understanding of The Five Practices of Exemplary Leadership model by reading about students who demonstrate the leadership behaviors embedded in the model. The stories in the book are intended to both inform and inspire you.

Leadership isn't telling people what to do. It's painting a picture of an exciting possibility of how we can achieve a common goal.
— ANTHONY BIANCHI

The Five Practices of Exemplary Leadership build on each other. When leaders Model the Way, they have a clearly defined set of values and encourage those in their group to also define the values they will share and live by. Leaders strive to align their actions with the values they hold. They also guide the group to take action based on clearly identified shared values. A logical progression from this values-based foundation is to then envision how things could be better. This is the heart of Inspire a Shared Vision: leaders offer their image of the future to others as an invitation to join together and pursue a better place, taking into consideration others' dreams and aspirations as well.

UNDERSTAND AND PRACTICE THE LEADERSHIP BEHAVIORS OF INSPIRE A SHARED VISION

The following activities will help you explore and deepen your understanding of the leadership behaviors that connect to Inspire a Shared Vision. Focus on one behavior at a time and identify opportunities to demonstrate that behavior more often.

NOTE

For each leadership behavior, you will find two iterations of the statement that describes the behavior: (1) the statement as it appears in the Student LPI and (2) how the behavior is described in the student report that is generated from taking the Student LPI.

> "I look ahead and communicate about what I believe will affect us in the future."
> (*Student LPI Report*: "Looks ahead and communicates future.")

1. Describe how you envision the group eight months from now (or a selected period of time that might fit your school year or other calendar period). What changes do you see the group having experienced? What would you hope the group would have accomplished? How do you see the group members having grown through their involvement? What actions need to be taken to make the group relevant? What other significant things do you see changing in the group?

At the end of the academic year (or other defined period), I envision the group to be:

The group would have accomplished (i.e., how it would have been productive in meeting its purpose):

Three important changes I see the group having experienced are:

A.

B.

C.

The group members have grown by:

Actions we need to take to make the group relevant:

Other changes I imagine the group having:

2. What are three things you see that the group will need to focus on in the future related to its purpose? How will you describe to the group why those matter and what the group needs to do about them?

In order for the group to better meet or live up to its purpose in the next eight months, the group will need to do these three things:

A:

This is important to the group because:

B:

This is important to the group because:

C:

This is important to the group because:

3.   How can you talk about your vision of the future with the group on a regular basis? What does "regular basis" mean to you, and why is it important to talk about your vision? Describe the commitment you will make to do this.

My vision of the future for the group is:

I need to share this vision with the group regularly because:

The more involvement people have in creating the vision and making it their own, the more support the leader will have.

—DENA JONES

To do this, I will (describe specifically what you will do and how often):

INSPIRE
A SHARED
VISION

"I am upbeat and positive when talking about what we can accomplish." (*Student LPI Report:* "Is upbeat and positive.")

1. Talk with three fellow members of the group and ask them how they perceive your interests and commitment toward what the group is doing. You can ask how they feel when you talk about what the group can do. If they are unable to describe that, use this as an opportunity to talk to them about what you could say that would make them more committed and interested in helping the group accomplish what it can.

I will ask three group members how they perceive my commitment in helping the group realize its vision. I will do this by

These are the questions I will ask: (a) What do you feel when I am sharing with the group what I think the group can do or become? (b) How committed do you feel to the group or its purpose? (c) What do you need to become more committed to the group? (d) How can you help you the group accomplish what it wants to do? List below what you have learned after talking with each person:

A.

B.

C.

2. Ask group members what makes them feel good about being involved in the meetings or projects (i.e., what gives them energy and excitement) and what makes them feel drained (as if being involved is more of a chore or burden).

I will talk to five group members to see what excites them about the group and what drains their energy from the group:

Person	What Is Exciting?	What Is Burdensome?
A.		
B.		

Person	What Is Exciting?	What Is Burdensome?
C.		
D.		
E.		

INSPIRE
A SHARED
VISION

> "I speak with passion about the higher purpose and meaning of what we are doing."
> (*Student LPI Report:* "Communicates purpose and meaning.")

1. Describe in a sentence or two what you think is the ultimate purpose of a group in which you are involved. Share that statement with the group and discuss what others see that is different and that is the same. Talk with the group about how their daily work contributes to that purpose.

I believe that the purpose of this group is:

In the past two weeks, I have shared this statement with _____ members of the group. _____ members generally or totally agree with what I've told them. _____ members generally do not agree or do not understand what I've told them. Here's what I will talk about each day with those who don't agree or understand to see how I can help them have a more meaningful experience with the group:

2. Using what you found out in item 1, define the shared understanding of what the vision of the group is. Below the purpose statement you provided, ask each member to write one or two sentences about what they do (or will do) in the group to contribute to meeting that purpose. You can have them do this anonymously or identify themselves. Share the final list with the entire group. Is anything missing that you or others need to find within the group that will help the group achieve its purpose? How accurately is the group aligning its actions with the values based on this vision? What do you need to better understand where and why the group might lack congruence? What actions can you and members of the group take to affirm others' values and strengthen the group's purpose?

Based on what you have learned from those who know, agree with, and understand the purpose of the group and those who do not, what, if anything, would you revise about the purpose you stated to make it more clear? (Keep in mind that you are not changing what you think the purpose of the group is in order to match the group's members unless you feel this is necessary). You are, in essence, clarifying how you think about the purpose of the group.

After you collected written responses from group members on how they see the purpose of the group what, if anything, changes in your definition?

How will you communicate what you have learned to the group?

3. List as many things as you can that you specifically did in the past two weeks to work toward the group's purpose. How did you share or talk about those experiences with others?

Given your responses and action to the experiences and questions you have asked of yourself and others for Inspire a Shared Vision, list any specific actions you took that helped the group clarify or get closer to realizing their vision:

A.

B.

C.

D.

E.

The key was making the vision of our success a joint process because we all came to believe that we could do it.

—FILIP MOROVICH

Describe how you shared your greater understanding about the group's vision with the group members:

INSPIRE
A SHARED
VISION

"I talk with others about how their own interests can be met by working toward a common goal." (*Student LPI Report:* "Shows others how their interests can be realized.")

1.   On a scale of 1 to 10 (with 1 being not very well and 10 being very well), how well would you say you know other members of the group in terms of what they hope to gain from being in the group? Circle the number on the number line. Given this score, what are ways you can engage more with everyone or with the few whom you might not know well?

I know what members of the group hope to gain from being in the group:

1	2	3	4	5	6	7	8	9	10
Not very well									Very well

These are the specific steps I can do to move my score more toward a 10:

2.   What would you specifically ask others in order to learn about their goals and reasons for being in the group? What questions will help you learn about the vision they have for themselves while in the organization? What questions would help you understand their vision for the group as a whole?

To improve my score on question 1, I would ask the following questions of the group members to get to know better their reasons for being a member of this group:

A.

B.

C.

D.

E.

To better understand what the members of the group hope to accomplish and how they hope to grow by being a member of this group, I would ask the following questions:

A.

B.

C.

D.

E.

To better understand what vision the group members have for the group itself, I would ask the following questions:

A.

B.

C.

D.

E.

3. In your next meeting with an organization in which you're involved, spend a few minutes listening to what people in the group say is important to them. Summarize what you learned from listening to them:

On this date, _____, I spoke with the group to learn more about what is important to the members in terms of their involvement in the group. In this conversation, I learned:

4. Using the summary of what you learned, identify and talk with individual members about how they might contribute to what is important to the group based on their individual needs, interests, and strengths.

Based on what I have learned from my responses and actions for the previous three questions, I can take the following actions to better help others contribute to and experience from the group:

A.

B.

C.

D.

E.

> "I talk with others about a vision of how things could be even better in the future."
> (*Student LPI Report:* "Talks about how the future could be better.")

1.   Think about when you had a conversation with others recently about how the group could be in the future. How did that conversation go? What was the reaction of those in the group? Did they seem excited? Were they eager to start? Were they hesitant? What else? How do you think the conversation contributed to the reactions you saw?

If you haven't ever talked about how the group could be in the future, why not? What kept you from sharing your thoughts?

If you have had a conversation about how the organization could be and some time has passed, how did this vision influence how the group operated, functioned, succeeded, or was challenged or failed, or changed in some way:

Was this vision one that you shared with the group on a regular basis? If yes, how did you do this? If no, what kept you from doing so?

2.   Given the impact you described, what strategies can you employ to keep the group focused on its vision on a regular basis?

3. As new members join groups you are part of, what can you and other members do to help them become a part of the group's vision? Why is this important for new members to know about the vision for the group?

> "I describe to others in our organization what we should be capable of accomplishing." (*Student LPI Report:* "Describes ideal capabilities.")

1. When was the last time you spoke to a group you're leading about what you envision it doing in the future? What specifically did you say about what you envision?

We discussed our future as a group on _____ and the vision I/we described was:

2. Describe the concept of "ideal." If you had a vision for a group you are leading that was "ideal," what would *ideal* mean to you? How close to ideal is your vision for the group? If the group was an ideal or model group of its kind, it would be:

At this point, I would say our group is _____ % of the ideal group it needs to be.

3. If you haven't had a conversation with this group in which you talk about what it is capable of, list three to five things you think the group can do to make a difference. How will you describe these possibilities to the members? Write out a statement that will help you express what you believe the possibilities to be.

This group can make a greater difference if it focused on doing these things:

A:

To specifically describe to the group the things we need to do, I would say:

B:

To specifically describe to the group the things we need to do, I would say:

C:

To specifically describe to the group the things we need to do, I would say:

D:

To specifically describe to the group the things we need to do, I would say:

E:

To specifically describe to the group the things we need to do, I would say:

FURTHER ACTIONS TO IMPROVE IN INSPIRE A SHARED VISION

A list of suggested actions follows that you can try in order to Inspire a Shared Vision more often. Some of the specific leadership behaviors in the Student LPI that are influenced by these actions are listed by number following each suggestion (see Appendix A for the complete list of Student LPI statements and behaviors).

1. Talk with an advisor, coach, or staff member or teacher about how you might think of some new ways in which you can help a group look at its vision more clearly and about different ways in which the group might better align with its vision. (2, 12, 22, 27)

2. Take stock of what you get excited about with your group. How does that excitement influence what you can do to connect with others in the group? What conversations will help others see the possibilities you can explore together to better realize your vision? (7, 12, 22, 27)

3.   Imagine that it's one year from today. What is different about the group? What has it accomplished? How is the group better off than it was a year ago? Why? (2, 7, 12)

4.   Talk with individuals in your group about their hopes and aspirations for the organization. Figure out what is shared and how those things relate to what you personally envision for the group. Think about how the group's vision is or is not in alignment with what others in the group think. (7, 12, 17)

5.   The next several times you meet or talk with people in your group gatherings, listen for the language they use. Is it tentative or noncommittal, such as, "We'll try," or, "We could/should"? Can you make sure that it is more positive and committed such as, "We will!"? (7, 22, 27)

6.   As a leader, ask yourself, "Am I in this role because of something I can or want to accomplish for myself?" or, "Am I here to do something for others?" Are you working to lead the group toward the group's shared vision or your own agenda? (12, 17, 27)

7.   Sharing a vision requires clarity and confidence. If it is difficult for you to talk emphatically and confidently to a group, look for multiple opportunities, such as other student groups that involve public speaking, to speak in front of people no matter what the purpose. The more often you do this, the more confident and comfortable you will be in speaking situations. (22, 27)

8.   Who are other leaders you find inspiring? Study and read about them to see how they communicate their vision for those they lead. What is it about what and how they say things that stands out to you and is the reason for your inspiration? Think about how you can learn from what they say and do. (2, 12, 22, 27)

ACTIVITIES TO LEARN ABOUT AND APPLY INSPIRE A SHARED VISION

Activity 4.1

The Dream Sheet

Overview

This activity can help you think about the vision you need to have for yourself as a leader. We are asking student leaders to think about how they define a vision for themselves, not how they define a vision for their group.

Objectives

After completing this activity you will be able to:

*   Reflect on what is needed to communicate a vision
*   Develop a clear vision with the ability to articulate it to others

Materials and Equipment

Dream Sheet worksheet (Figure 4.1)

Process

1. If you could dream about whatever it would take to make you an effective leader, what would your dream look like? In other words, when you see yourself as the most effective leader you could be, what does that look like for you?

2. Using the Dream Sheet, write a response to each of the following questions within the context of how you can see yourself as an effective leader. Write down the dreams and aspirations you have for yourself as a leader. Answer each question as thoroughly as you can. You have thirty minutes. Begin with this overarching question: "What would I look like as an effective leader?" Follow with the remaining seven clouds:

   1. To begin living my dream, I have to experience . . .
   2. I have to learn . . .
   3. I have to sacrifice . . .
   4. I have to risk . . .
   5. To realize my dream I need . . .
   6. Who else can or will need to play a role in my dream . . . ?
   7. What else do I need to do?

Activity 4.2

Come Join Me on Vacation

Overview

This activity helps you practice engaging others with your vision of the future. The notion of creating a compelling vision that inspires and drives people to action can seem daunting. But like anything else you want to master, it takes practice. This exercise helps you see that you have the basic skills to create a compelling vision and that to be successful, you need only to work to understand others and practice, practice, practice.

Objectives

After completing this exercise, you will be able to:

- Articulate a desirable image of the future for others
- Understand that your vision began from your own heart, passion, and values and then connected to the values and passions of others

Figure 4.1 The Dream Sheet

Dreaming Leads to Your Vision

If you could dream anything about becoming an effective leader, what would it be?

Use this dream sheet to write down your dreams for yourself as a leader. Use dream cloud 1 to define what kind of a leader you want to become. What would it look like? What would you be doing? Then use the other dream clouds to define how you might begin working toward this. What do you need to do to learn, experience, risk, or sacrifice to make your dream, your vision, come to life?

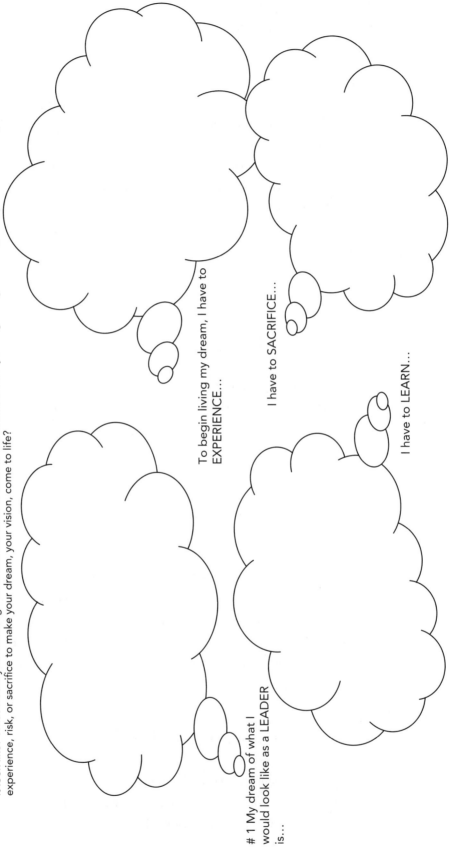

To begin living my dream, I have to EXPERIENCE...

I have to SACRIFICE...

I have to LEARN...

1 My dream of what I would look like as a LEADER is...

Dreaming Leads to Vision

If you saw yourself as the most EFFECTIVE LEADER you could be, what would that look like?

To REALIZE my dream I need...

Who ELSE can/will need to play a role in my dream...?

What else do I NEED TO DO...?

I have to RISK...

Process

1. Think about a place where you have gone on vacation and would love to return to with your friends.

2. Close your eyes and think about this place. What do you feel, hear, taste, or smell? What makes you want to smile? Open your eyes and take some short notes about what you experienced.

3. Invite the person you are partnered with (or a small group) to spend time with you at this vacation place. Think about the people you are speaking to. What do they like to do? How do they like to spend their free time? Using your own enthusiasm and your insight into these other people, invite them in a way that will inspire them to join you and spend time in this place. Rotate through each person.

Activity 4.3

Movie Activity: *Invictus*

The Five Practices of Exemplary Leadership show up in many movies. This activity features selected clips that illustrate the use of Inspire a Shared Vision. Included is a brief synopsis of the film, a description of the clips that showcase the practice, and then a series of questions for you to answer or consider.

Movies are a great way to spark your creative thinking about how the Five Practices show up in real life. While the clips listed here are clear examples of Inspire a Shared Vision, look for examples of any of the other practices or leadership behaviors.

Movie

2009. Director: Clint Eastwood
Screenplay: Anthony Peckham
Distribution: Warner Bros. Pictures
Rated PG-13 for brief strong language (this element is not in the scenes in this activity)

This movie is based on a book written by John Carlin, *Playing the Enemy*, about Nelson Mandela's work in his first year as president of South Africa to unite the country in the wake of apartheid.

Synopsis

Invictus is based on a true story about Nelson Mandela a few years after his release from his twenty-six-year imprisonment. Elected president of South Africa in 1994, he has a tremendous challenge as he works to heal and unite a country after years of apartheid. He decides to take advantage of the upcoming 1995 Rugby World Cup that South Africa is hosting and hopes to draw people together through the universally understood language of sport. The South Africa Springboks have less than a year to prepare for the World Cup and are playing in the World Cup only because they are the host nation. The mostly white team has long been a symbol of the racial division and hatred in the country, which makes its ability to serve as the catalyst for country unity even more challenging. President Mandela hopes he can engage the captain of the team, François Pienaar, so that he can lead the team to a World Cup victory, thus helping the country to unite. This film tells the story of how, even in times of great conflict and struggle, leaders who have a clear vision and drive to make things better do make a difference.

Scene Descriptions

The following two scene descriptions illustrate Inspire a Shared Vision. You can view these scenes as individual clips, stopping to discuss them in between, or as a collective sequence with discussion afterward.

Theme: Look to the Future. Begins in chapter 3 of the DVD at approximately 0:08:24 to 0:11:53.

> In this scene depicting the first time President Mandela addresses the staff of the president's office after his election, he shares his observation that many from the previous administration are packing their offices in preparation to leave as he takes office. He tells his audience of their right to make that choice; however, he hopes they will stay and help serve the country. The president describes what he needs and expects of those who stay and tells of the importance and necessity of their work.

Theme: Need to Exceed. Begins in chapter 10 of the DVD at approximately 0:45:29 to 0:51:16. Begin a chapter earlier to set the context for the scene.

> President Mandela has invited the captain of South Africa's rugby team, François Pienaar, to his office for tea. He talks with François about his philosophy on leadership and how he tries to get others to do their best. He talks about inspiration and what it should do. President Mandela shares how he survived his prison confinement. This scene shows how two different leaders create their visions for those they lead.

> In a follow-up scene after his visit with the president, François shares his vision with the team. His inspiration and clarity from the president's message is evident when he tells the team, "Times change and we need to change as well."

Leadership Lessons from *Invictus*

Discussion Questions for "Look to the Future"

1. What examples of Inspire a Shared Vision do you see in this scene?
2. If you were on the president's staff, how do you think you would have felt after hearing his message? What parts of his message stood out to you?

Discussion Questions for "Need to Exceed"

1. When President Mandela spoke with François in his office and asked about his philosophy of leadership, how do you see his vision for the country coming across in what he hopes François can achieve through rugby and the World Cup? What else did you notice the president doing?

2. How does François' follow-up meeting with the team mirror the challenges that President Mandela faces with the country? What do you see François doing to share his vision?

Discussion Question for Both Scenes

1. What other practices and leadership behaviors did you notice in these scenes?

CONNECT INSPIRE A SHARED VISION TO MODULE 8: PERSONAL LEADERSHIP JOURNAL

The Personal Leadership Journal is available to help you shape your ongoing learning about each practice. There are three sections:

Section 1: Complete this section once you have had an opportunity to do a thorough review of your Student LPI report. You may be asked to complete this outside the classroom or formal workshop time, though that choice is up to your instructor. If you have not taken the Student LPI, complete this after you have a good understanding of Inspire a Shared Vision and the behaviors aligned with that practice.

Section 2: Complete this section after you have taken action. It will help guide you to your next targeted action step.

Section 3: Use this section as a support tool for your ongoing and independent exploration of Inspire a Shared Vision.

MODULE 5

Challenge the Process

PRACTICE SUMMARY

Challenge provides the opportunity for greatness. People do their best when there's a chance to change the way things are. Maintaining the status quo simply breeds mediocrity. Leaders seek and accept challenging opportunities to test their abilities. They motivate others as well to exceed their self-perceived limits and seize the initiative to make something meaningful happen. Leaders treat every assignment as an adventure.

Most innovations come not from leaders themselves but from the people closest to the work. They also come from "outsight"—the way exemplary leaders look outward for good ideas everywhere. Leaders promote external communication and then listen, take advice, and learn.

Progress is made incrementally, not in giant leaps. Exemplary leaders move forward in small steps with little victories. They turn adversity into advantage and setbacks into successes. They persevere with grit and determination.

Leaders venture out. They test and they take risks with bold ideas. And because risk taking involves mistakes and failure, leaders accept and grow from the inevitable disappointments. They treat these as opportunities to learn and grow.

We highly recommend you read *The Student Leadership Challenge* book to deepen your understanding of The Five Practices of Exemplary Leadership model by reading about students who demonstrate the leadership behaviors embedded in the model. The stories in the book are intended to both inform and inspire you.

When I did question the status quo, when I did come up with innovative ideas, when I followed through with the changes I suggested, got feedback, understood my mistakes, learned from them and was open to improvements I won the respect of the people around me.
— VARUN MUNDRA

UNDERSTAND AND PRACTICE THE LEADERSHIP BEHAVIORS OF CHALLENGE THE PROCESS

The following activities will help you explore and deepen your understanding of the leadership behaviors that connect to Challenge the Process. Focus on one behavior at a time, and identify opportunities to demonstrate that behavior more often.

NOTE For each behavior, you will find two iterations of the statement that describes the behavior: (1) the statement as it appears in the Student LPI and (2) the way the behavior is described in the student report that is generated from taking the Student LPI.

CHALLENGE
THE PROCESS

> "I look for ways to develop and challenge my skills and abilities." (*Student LPI Report:* "Challenges skills and abilities.")

1. What are three skills or abilities you want to learn or develop that would help you be a better leader?

A.

B.

C.

2. Where can you find a group, activity, or project that might offer you the chance to learn specific new skills or strengthen ones you have now?

3. Who has the individual skill set you desire? Can you talk with that person to learn from his or her experience? How did this person go about developing those skills and acquiring those talents?

I learned that in all environments when things don't work properly you shouldn't just accept it as being just the way it is. There are in fact massive opportunities to shine as an innovative person.
—JADE LUI

CHALLENGE
THE PROCESS

4. How will you evaluate your progress in developing your skills? Who could you talk with that would give you feedback about your current level of relevant skills and abilities?

"I search for innovative ways to improve what we are doing." (*Student LPI Report:* "Searches for innovative ways to improve.")

1. Ask your group to identify three things they think get in the way of their ability to be even more successful. Come up with some actions the group can take to address those inhibitors.

A.

B.

C.

2. Taking the responses from the previous question, look for other groups at your school or a similar organization that you think do those things well. Spend time talking with others in those groups to learn what they do in similar circumstances. Find out how they overcame their obstacles, and discuss with your colleagues how your group can use those lessons learned.

A.

B.

C.

3. State the specific actions you will take to help your group implement what you learned about other groups to overcome obstacles the group or your group is facing:

A.

B.

C.

CHALLENGE
THE PROCESS

"I take initiative in experimenting with the way things can be done." (*Student LPI Report:* "Takes initiative in experimenting.")

1.   What would it take for you to help your group feel comfortable about trying something new?

2.   In what activity could you encourage your group to do something different from what they have done in the past that would improve the activity?

3.   How can you help others feel safe in expressing their ideas for trying something new?

Our goal seemed enor-mous; so we broke it down into parts and gave one part to each member.

—RICHARD CABRAL

4.   What statements or language can you encourage your group to remove from their vocabulary that will enable them to try a new experiment?

CHALLENGE
THE PROCESS

"I make sure that big projects we undertake are broken down into smaller and doable parts." (*Student LPI Report:* "Breaks projects into smaller doable portions.")

1.   What are three pieces of a large project for which you can establish milestones with your group to meet in the upcoming _____ (describe the time frames

for any or all of the portions of the project that best suit your group's meeting and work schedules)?

Week

1.

2.

3.

Month

1.

2.

3.

Quarter/Semester

1.

2.

3.

Year

1.

2.

3.

2.   How will you help your group determine if these milestones were met? If you do meet them, do you know what you did for that to happen? If you don't meet them, do you know what caused that?

3. Identify a new project, area, or initiative the group will work on, and set a reasonable number of goals for key parts of that activity. Follow the same process given in items 1 and 2 to determine your progress toward meeting your goals. As you see the group grow, extend the goals.

CHALLENGE
THE PROCESS

> "I look for ways that others can try out new ideas and methods." (*Student LPI Report:* "Helps others try out new ideas.")

1. Where can you go to get some new ideas or learn how to do something differently from the way you do it now?

2. Look at something you are doing now that is challenging for you or your group. Write down three actions different from what you are doing now that might address that challenge:

A.

B.

C.

3.   Look at something that your group is doing well or is well known for. Write down three actions, in addition to what you are doing now, that might improve on or even expand on this success:

A.

B.

C.

4.   How can you make it easy for others to try out new things and take a risk? How can you let them know that it is all right for them to experiment and teach them that from these trials, the group can gain greater understanding of what can be accomplished?

CHALLENGE
THE PROCESS

When things don't go as we expected, I ask, "What can we learn from this experience?" (*Student LPI Report*: "Asks, 'What can we learn?'")

1.   What experience did you recently have that didn't go as you expected?

2. What are one to three specific things you learned from this experience that will benefit you in the future?

A.

B.

C.

3. For each item you just identified, write how you can use what you learned when you have another opportunity to experiment:

A.

B.

C.

The similarity that most stuck out was that each person's story was about having to overcome uncertainty and fear in order to achieve his or her best.

—KATHERINE WINKEL

4. Are there ways you have come to think about mistakes that have made you resilient? How can you share your own experiences with mistakes and learn from them with others you work with?

FURTHER ACTIONS TO IMPROVE IN CHALLENGE THE PROCESS

A list of suggested actions follows that you can try out in order to improve in Challenge the Process. Some of the specific leadership behaviors in the Student LPI that are influenced by these actions are listed by number following each suggestion (see Appendix A for the complete list of Student LPI statements and behaviors).

1. Make a list of tasks that you perform that are related to your various leadership activities. For each task, ask yourself, "Why am I doing this? Why am I doing it this way? Can this task be eliminated or done significantly better?" Based on your responses, do you see where you can develop other skills? Identify those skills, and look for applicable opportunities within your leadership activities where you can work to develop the skills you have identified. (3, 8)

2. Make a list of the things your group does that are basically done the same way as they have always been done before. For each routine, ask, "Are we doing this at our best?" If yes, then carry on! If no, look for ways to change to make it better. (8, 18, 28)

3. Continue to observe and learn about what makes other leaders successful, and then think about your own skills. Which skills do you see those leaders having that you don't have? Perhaps you believe you have those skills but need to strengthen them. Talk to those individuals and ask for their suggestions on what you could do to get stronger. If you don't have that opportunity, write down the skills or abilities you want to work on and ask an advisor, teacher, coach, or student life staff member to help you find places at your school or organization where you can develop those skills. (3, 13)

4. Ask others in your group what frustrates them about the organization. Make a commitment to change three of the most frequently mentioned items that are frustrating people and probably hindering the group's success. (13, 18)

5. Identify a process in your group that's not working, and take action to fix it. Learn from your experience. (18, 28)

6. Experiment by doing something you are not currently doing that will benefit your group—perhaps something new you can do within a project or event you are already working

on. You might find something new you can do together that can meet a goal of your group. Make your experiments small, and learn from them for future larger experiments. (8, 28)

7. Eliminate "fire hosing" (throwing water on every new idea without giving it consideration). Remove from your group's vocabulary the "That'll never work" phrase or "The problem with that is . . ." At the very least, give new ideas the benefit of discussion and reflection. Recognize that even if the first idea isn't valuable, it might lead to others that are. (8, 18, 28)

8. Call or visit your counterparts in other organizations at your school, another school or group, or another community (both those in groups similar to yours and different from yours). Find out what they are doing and learn from their successes and challenges. Copy what they do well, and use their failures as a guide for improvement. (13, 28)

9. Set achievable goals. Tell people what the key milestones are and review them frequently so that you and they can easily see progress. (23)

10. Eliminate the phrase, "That's the way we did it last year," from all discussions. Use the results of past programs or projects to learn from, but don't fall into the trap of doing something the same way simply because it's easier. (8, 23, 28)

ACTIVITIES TO LEARN ABOUT AND APPLY CHALLENGE THE PROCESS

Activity 5.1

We Need More Parking

Overview

This activity is a small group exercise that challenges you to look for alternative solutions to the work you do as a leader and help you practice the behaviors associated with Challenge the Process. This activity provides the opportunity to practice the concept of outsight and helps you learn about searching outside your group or team for innovative ways to improve. In this activity, you learn about experimenting through idea generation and have the chance to think about how different ideas can influence various outcomes.

Objectives

After completing this exercise you will be able to:

- Understand and apply the concept of outsight to use with their groups to find innovative ways to improve
- Take the initiative in experimenting
- Learn the impact on change from asking, "What can we learn?"

Process

1. You will form small groups of five or six students each, with each group having the same number of students. Each group identifies itself by an identifying number (e.g., group 1, 2, 3).

2. Each group is to generate possible solutions to improve or resolve a situation your facilitator has identified, perhaps addressing the perennial problem of how to get more parking.

3. In this first round, each group has thirty minutes to identify ten solutions, write each one on a slip of paper, and place them in a group envelope with the number of the group on it. Exchange envelopes among groups.

4. In this next round, each group reviews the solutions in the envelope it receives and briefly discusses them. (This is not an evaluation, simply a review of the original group's ideas). If there is an idea that isn't clear to any group member in this round, the group can ask the originating group for more information or clarification. Each group identifies three additional solutions to the original list of your neighboring group. It writes these on three additional strips of paper. It has twenty minutes to do so.

5. Each group identifies its top three potential solutions in the envelope it is holding, and then all groups share their choices.

Activity 5.2

Take It One Step at a Time

Overview

This reflective exercise helps break large challenges into small, actionable steps that generate small wins. It can also involve the use of outsight by including pairings or small group work.

Objectives

You will be able to:

- Use core elements of Challenge the Process to generate clear, actionable next steps
- Experience the outsight provided by a peer who is unfamiliar with the challenge

Process

1. Create three sections on a blank tablet or piece of paper and label them:
   - Current Challenge
   - Perceived Obstacles
   - Small Step/Small Win Opportunity

2. Describe the obstacle in the first section with as much detail as needed for someone else to understand the situation.

3. List the obstacles you believe are in the way of making progress past that challenge.

4. Identify one small thing you believe you can do to make some progress, even if it doesn't completely resolve the problem.

5. In pairs or small groups, share your example, but do not reveal your small step/small win ideas. Let the other person offer ideas from a fresh perspective; then you can share your own ideas.

Activity 5.3

Movie Activity: *Apollo 13*

The Five Practices of Exemplary Leadership show up in many movies. This activity features selected clips that illustrate the use of Challenge the Process. Included is a brief synopsis of the film, a description of the clips that showcase the practice, followed by a series of questions for you to answer or consider.

Movies are a great way to spark your creative thinking about how The Five Practices show up in real life. While the clips listed here are clear examples of Challenge the Process, look for examples of any of the other practices or leadership behaviors.

Movie

1995. Director: Ron Howard

Screenplay: William Broyles Jr. and Al Reinert

Distribution: Universal Pictures

Rated PG for language and emotional intensity

This movie is based on the book with the same title cowritten by Jeffrey Kluger and James Lovell Jr., one of the astronauts on the *Apollo* space flight to the moon in 1970. *Apollo 13* was the third U.S. space mission to put a man on the moon.

Synopsis

In the film, the spacecraft *Apollo 13* suffers a massive explosion while on its way to the moon in a section of the craft where the oxygen tanks are located that puts the lives of the three astronauts at risk: James A. Lovell Jr., the commander; John L. Swigert Jr., the command module pilot; and Fred W. Haise Jr., the lunar module pilot. For nearly six days, the ship and its crew are handicapped by the explosion and are without a plan to return to Earth safely. The NASA space program is still young and has never before encountered this situation.

Scene Descriptions

The following two scenes illustrate Challenge the Process. You can view these scenes as individual clips, stopping to discuss them in between, or as a collective sequence with discussion afterward. In each scene, you will find examples that you can use to supplement the conversation about leadership and Challenge the Process (as well as other leadership practices).

Theme: Failure Is Not an Option. Begins in chapter 32 on the DVD at approximately 1:19:42 to 1:21:07.

NASA realizes that the carbon monoxide levels in the astronauts' command module are becoming dangerously toxic. If the levels continue to rise, all three astronauts will die. Lowering the levels requires a special system to filter out the carbon monoxide, but the existing system is not working as designed because of the damage to the craft. The on-the-ground NASA chief urgently brings together some of his staff to identify and resolve the problem. The leader of that team brings an assortment of random parts and items that they know the astronauts can access on the spacecraft. The team must find a creative way to construct a functioning filter system in order to reduce the carbon monoxide levels and keep the astronauts alive. In essence, they must find a solution by successfully putting a square peg in a round hole.

Theme: More Power Needed. Begins at chapter 44 on the DVD at approximately 1:47:50 to 1:50:50.

One of the on-the-ground astronauts is working to develop a plan to provide the power the command module needs to reenter the Earth's atmosphere. The damage to the command module is significant: many of the batteries and power systems have been damaged. The crew needs most of the onboard systems fully functional so they can safely reenter the atmosphere and land. In this scene, pay attention to what the on-the-ground astronaut, Thomas Mattingly, does to determine a solution to the power problem.

Leadership Lessons from *Apollo 13*

Discussion Questions for "Failure Is Not an Option"

1. What did you see happening in the conversation with the NASA director before the team develops a solution?

2. What did Gene Krantz (the mission control flight director) do to help the team craft a solution?

3. How do you think Krantz's interaction made the team feel? How might that have affected their performance?

4. What are the team's first steps in working to find a solution?

Discussion Questions for "More Power Needed"

1. Although Mattingly was seemingly working on a solution alone in the capsule, he also had a team helping him. What did you see him doing that worked to define a solution with the help of his team members?

2. What examples did you notice of learning from mistakes?

Discussion Questions for Both Scenes

1. What risks were apparent in either of these situations, and how did the teams and individuals address them?

2. How might past experiences have influenced the work either group was doing?

CONNECT CHALLENGE THE PROCESS TO MODULE 8: PERSONAL LEADERSHIP JOURNAL

The Personal Leadership Journal is available to help you shape your ongoing learning about each practice. There are three sections:

Section 1: Complete this section once you have had an opportunity to do a thorough review of your Student LPI report. You may be asked to complete this outside the classroom or formal workshop time, though that choice is up to your instructor. If you have not taken the Student LPI, complete this after you have a good understanding of Challenge the Process and the behaviors aligned with that practice.

Section 2: Complete this section after you have taken action. It will help guide you on to your next targeted action step.

Section 3: Use this section as a support tool for your ongoing and independent exploration of Challenge the Process.

MODULE 6
Enable Others to Act

PRACTICE SUMMARY

Leaders know that they cannot achieve great success alone. They know it take partners to make extraordinary things happen on teams, in small groups, or in larger organizations. Exemplary student leaders create an atmosphere of mutual respect and trust that allows people to rely on each other and work hard together. They build groups that feel connected and help people take ownership for the group's success.

Getting people to work together begins with establishing and then sustaining trust. It also requires a clear set of cooperative goals based on the values and the vision the group shares. Leaders understand how being trustworthy is the reciprocal of trusting others. They focus on "we," not "I."

Leaders realize that power is an expandable resource and strive to make each person feel empowered. They realize that empowering others is essentially the process of turning followers into leaders themselves. Great leaders, in other words, create more leaders.

Leaders understand that the process of strengthening others starts with the leader. They allow others to grow by letting them work on tasks that are critical to the success of the group and choose how they will take on their tasks. Leaders ensure that individual efforts are visible and recognized by others, and they facilitate the connection to others for support.

We highly recommend you read *The Student Leadership Challenge* book to deepen your understanding of The Five Exemplary Leadership Practices model by reading about students who demonstrate the leadership behaviors embedded in the model. The stories in the book are intended to both inform and inspire you.

UNDERSTAND AND PRACTICE THE LEADERSHIP BEHAVIORS OF ENABLE OTHERS TO ACT

It wasn't my personal best. It was our personal best.
—SUSAN COHEN

The following activities will help you explore and deepen your understanding of the leadership behaviors that connect to Enable Others to Act. Focus on one behavior at a time, and identify opportunities to demonstrate that behavior more often.

NOTE

For each behavior, you will find two iterations of the statement that describes the behavior: (1) the statement as it appears in the Student LPI and (2) how the behavior is described in the student report that is generated from taking the Student LPI.

> "I treat others with dignity and respect." (*Student LPI Report:* "Treats others with respect.")

1. Describe the responsibility you think a leader has for respecting and valuing everyone in the group. How is that different from liking everyone in the group?

Where does the responsibility lie in working to establish effective, productive working relationships in a group? Why do you think that?

Describe the difference between having relationships that are effective and productive and those that are social and friendly. Are these mutually exclusive? Why or why not?

What is the role of the leader (and also the benefit or lack thereof) in facilitating relationships?

2. If you don't take the time and energy to get to know others in your group who are different from you, what impact would this have on the group? on the experience others have in the group?

What does a group sacrifice when the leader cannot connect with members of the group? What is the effect of this lack of connection on the:

Group?

Individual members?

3. Describe your general relationship with other members of your group. Are there any characteristics in your description that suggest you don't get along with or value others in the group?

Without naming names, think about the people you don't find yourself really connecting with. Why is that?

What could you do to strengthen that connection?

Are there any common grounds on which you and these other individuals could begin to develop a relationship?

Our team was able to create a notion of trust among one another, so that in any given situation, we could trust the other to do the right thing.
—JORDAN GOFF

ENABLE
OTHERS TO
ACT

"I actively listen to diverse points of view." (*Student LPI Report:* "Actively listens to diverse viewpoints.")

1. How do you react to others' points of view when you don't agree with them? How do those reactions affect your ability to lead and affect your relationships in and with the group? Describe what some of your recent reactions were when you didn't agree with others, particularly on significant issues (related to the group). Think about how you feel, what you think, and what your inner voice says, as well as what you actually say:

Can you think of any times when your reactions affected the group in any way? Describe those, and consider how your reactions might have affected others' participation or engagement at the moment, any changes in your short- or long-term relationships with others, or the impact on the productivity of the group:

2. Define what active listening means to you. Then describe a time when you really listened and responded to what another person had to offer. Describe another experience when you felt you weren't really interested in listening to what someone else in the group had to say. What were the different impacts on the interactions and relationships between you and the other person, and what were the subsequent impacts on the group? Define *active listening*. Then share your definition with one or two other people. How closely do they match or differ?

When was there a time that you were totally uninterested in what someone else in the group was saying?

When was there a time when you were engaged in what someone else was saying?

What impact do you think you had on the group based on two situations such as those?

In order to build collaboration you need to let go of responsibility and give others a chance to take it on. By entrusting others with responsibility you are letting them know you believe in them and that you have confidence that they can achieve it.
—ANA ABOITIZ

How does listening affect a leader's ability to enable (or not enable) others to be significant contributors to the group?

3. What are three things you think you can do to better listen to and understand another person's view that differs from yours? What might you gain from that point of view that would help you be a better leader? To become a better listener, I will:

A.

B.

C.

The differences I can make with my group as a result of being a better listener are:

ENABLE
OTHERS TO
ACT

> "I provide opportunities for others to take on leadership responsibilities." (*Student LPI Report:* "Provides leadership opportunities for others.")

1.   Identify opportunities in your group for others (without any concern for official titles or leadership positions) to take on leadership responsibility. Name five opportunities. Then expand the list to ten. What can you do to help others take advantage of these opportunities?

Five Opportunities

1.

2.

3.

4.

5.

Stretch yourself to find another five:

Five More Opportunities

6.

7.

8.

9.

10.

2.   What responsibility do you think a leader has in helping others in the group grow and develop as leaders? At what point do you think you can help someone do that? Do you instead say to yourself, "He can't be a leader," or, "She has to figure that out on her own"? Do you think leaders have a responsibility to develop other people to become leaders?

If your answer is yes, describe the role or responsibility you think a leader has to help others in the group develop as leaders themselves. If your answer is no, explain your reasoning.

3.   How would your role or day-to-day responsibilities or work as a leader change if others in the group took on more leadership? What opportunities would this provide you? What advantages do others taking on more leadership give the group?

If you had more people in the group who were able to take on greater leadership responsibilities within the group, how would that affect your role and work as a leader? What would be different?

What would be the same?

What would be easier?

What would be more difficult?

What new and different opportunities would arise for you if this happened?

How does the group benefit by this happening?

ENABLE
OTHERS TO
ACT

"I give others a great deal of freedom and choice in deciding how to do their work."
(*Student LPI Report*: "Gives people choice about how to do their work.")

1.   To what degree would you say you allow others to do their work as they see fit? To what degree do you feel you can let go completely and let others in the group take full responsibility for what they are doing? Describe the feelings you have when you do or don't do this.

Circle the number that matches the degree to which you let others have freedom to do their work:

1	2	3	4	5	6	7	8	9	10
Not very often									Frequently

What does it feel like when you:
Let go as completely as you can and allow others the freedom to do their work and assignments?

Don't let go and either micromanage or take over the assignment or work yourself?

What impact does either of the above actions have on the:
Group as a whole?

Individuals within the group?

2.   What are some specific things you can do to help members of the group develop a greater sense of confidence in the work that they do? If you did these things with each person in the group, what do you think would happen to (1) the individual and (2) the group? List four things you can do to help instill a greater sense of confidence in the people you are working with. State the action, and then write the name or initials of a person you could apply this action to:

	Action	Group Member
A.		
B.		
C.		
D.		

If you took these actions, what do you expect would happen to these people?

What are you expecting would happen to the group by you taking these actions?

3. If you are more likely to try to take on and do many things for the group yourself, think for a moment why that is. Write a reflection about:

When and why you take on responsibilities or tasks that others in the group could do:

What you are most concerned about or afraid of if you don't assume those responsibilities but provide them for others to assume:

4. What does success or failure mean for you and your group in the context of giving other people more freedom and choice in deciding how their work will be accomplished? Considering the situations you are reflecting about, if they didn't result in what you expect, what is the worst outcome that could happen? How will that affect you, the others in the group, and the group as a whole?

ENABLE
OTHERS TO
ACT

"I foster cooperative rather than competitive relationships among people I work with." (*Student LPI Report:* "Fosters cooperative relationships.")

1.   On a scale of 1 to 10, with 1 being low, how would you rate your sense of competitiveness? To what degree do you think competition should play into being a leader specifically as it relates to working with others in the group? Without letting go of or altering your sense of being competitive, describe how cooperation would differ in working with others when a leader takes on this characteristic more.

Competitiveness scale: Generally how would you describe your degree of competitiveness with others? Circle the number that applies.

1		2	3	4	5	6	7	8	9	10
Low Competitiveness										High Competitiveness

Describe how you think competitiveness should play into a leader's work with fellow members in the group:

How would you describe the advantages or benefits of cooperation over competitiveness when leaders work with others in their groups?

2.   When you find yourself being competitive with others in your group, what are the conversations, sharing of ideas, debates, and decisions like? How would they be any different if a more cooperative environment were present?

Describe the competitive environment in the group. For example, how does competition, if it exists, affect the group's conversations, ideas, debates, and decisions?

What would be different if people were more cooperative than competitive?

3.   What can you do as a leader to create a cooperative environment within your group? How would you describe the balance you think is necessary between cooperation and competitiveness? Is this any different when you are looking within the organization and its members or when you are looking at the greater purpose of the organization as it relates to other groups?

How would you describe your views on balancing competition with cooperation within a group?

What are the differences in this balance, if any, when you are considering the members of the group you're in versus your group perhaps in competition with another group? What is your role as a leader in influencing cooperation and competition?

4.   What circumstances, characteristics, or conditions do you think need to be present for a group to have a more cooperative environment? As a leader, what could you do to help create that environment?

ENABLE
OTHERS TO
ACT

> "I support the decisions that other people make on their own." (*Student LPI Report:* "Supports decisions other people make.")

1.   As a leader, what are your beliefs about letting others make decisions independently? How much latitude do you give them to make decisions? What kinds of decisions do you let them make? What tolerance for risk (the degree to which you think something will go wrong) do you have for others making decisions?

Circle the number that describes to what degree you let others make decisions independently:

1	2	3	4	5	6	7	8	9	10
Not very often									Frequently

Briefly describe the types of decisions you feel comfortable letting others do. Then give each one a number from 1 to 10 (see the number line below) to show the appropriate degree of risk.

A:

B:

C:

D:

1	2	3	4	5	6	7	8	9	10
Low Risk									High Risk

2. Look at how your behaviors affect other individuals. If you let others make decisions and support them in what they decide and give them freedom, how does that affect them as individuals? If you are more restrictive much of the time, how do you think that affects others as individuals? Be as specific as possible.

Are there patterns in the list of decisions you made and the risk tolerance you assigned in the previous activity? What can you do to become more comfortable in taking a greater degree of risk and allowing others to do so as well?

3. If you responded generally favorably that you let others make decisions, support them in what they decide, and give them freedom, what is the impact on the group? If you are more restrictive in most ways, how do you think that affects the group? Be as specific as you can be.

Describe as specifically as you can how letting others make decisions will affect the group (potentially positively and negatively):

FURTHER ACTIONS TO IMPROVE IN ENABLE OTHERS TO ACT

A list of suggested actions follows that you can try out in order to Enable Others to Act more often. Some of the specific leadership behaviors in the Student LPI that are influenced by these actions are listed by number following each suggestion (see Appendix A for the complete list of Student LPI statements and behaviors).

1. Teach others in your group to become leaders. Leaders bring others along to be leaders. Take some specific steps, perhaps starting with just one or two people, to help them develop their leadership abilities. (24, 29)

2. Make a point of encouraging others to take on important tasks or projects. Put the names forward of people in the group you believe would be well suited for a certain project. Similarly, talk with them about taking on a responsibility on behalf of the group, letting them know that you have confidence in their ability and judgment. (4, 14, 19, 24, 29)

3. Take another approach to item 2 by asking someone else to lead a group meeting or do a presentation so he or she can gain that experience (or any other experiences you identify). Then coach along the way to assist and support that person in this new capacity. (4, 14, 24, 29)

4. Give something up altogether that you do on a regular basis. Don't just give up something you don't want to do, but find someone in the group you think would grow from taking over this task as a regular responsibility. Be sure to let him or her know that you are not just getting rid of something you no longer care to do or think is critical; rather, explain how this represents an opportunity for this person to grow and develop. (4, 9, 19, 24, 29)

5. Identify someone at your school or in your community who is known as an exceptional leader. Contact that person and find out if you can follow or shadow him or her for a few hours to learn about how you can become better working with others. (4, 9, 14)

6. Improve relationships and develop a greater sense of trust with group members by doing something together outside regular group activities. Find ways to interact informally so you and they can build stronger bonds with each other. (4, 9, 14)

7. For the next two weeks, see how often you can replace "I" with "we" as you lead a group. Work to develop the philosophy and understanding that leadership is about the group or the team, not one individual. Every time you think about saying, "I'm going to . . . ," say instead, "We can do this . . ." (4, 9, 14, 29)

8. Ask an athletic coach if you can watch a practice or team meeting to see how he or she helps athletes develop new skills or identify and reach new goals. Think about how you can apply these lessons to the groups to which you belong. (4, 9)

ACTIVITIES TO LEARN ABOUT AND APPLY ENABLE OTHERS TO ACT

Activity 6.1

What Makes You Trust Someone?

Overview

This activity helps you examine the role of trust in effective leadership by evaluating your own level of trust in leaders you have known.

Objectives

After completing this exercise, you will be able to:

- Understand the importance of trust in effectively leading others
- Understand the potential impact on relationships within an organization or group
- Identify behaviors that promote trust

Process

1. Turn to the Trust Worksheet (Figure 6.1) in this exercise. Identify two people in leadership positions or roles—one you trust and one you do not trust. (They do not have to be from a current situation.)
2. Complete the worksheet. Under the "Trust" column, list the traits or behaviors that lead you to trust that person. Under the "Lack of Trust" column, list the traits or behaviors that prevent you from trusting that person. List the impact this person's behavior has on you and your work.
3. Once you have completed the worksheet, discuss your thoughts with others in your small groups. Make sure that everyone has a chance to contribute.
4. Identify common themes, and record them on a flip chart to share with the larger group. Looking at the collective themes from the flip charts, how do these themes relate to Commitment 7 from Enable Others to Act: Foster collaboration by building trust and facilitating relationships?

Figure 6.1 Trust Worksheet

Trust	Lack of Trust
List the traits or behaviors you believe helped you trust this person.	List the traits or behaviors you believe led you to not trust this person.
What impact did this person's behavior have on you and your work?	What impact did this person's behavior have on you and your work?

Activity 6.2

Blindfolded Square

Overview

This activity helps demonstrate how enabling (or disabling) others contributes to or takes away from the group's ability to reach their common goal.

Objectives

After you complete this exercise, you will:

- Understand the importance of sharing information when leading others
- Experience the importance of listening to others

- Identify behaviors that help others feel (or not feel) confident and capable
- Experience behaviors that contribute to (or hinder) high levels of group performance when faced with a new problem in unusual circumstances

Process

1. Form a large circle, with everyone an arm's length distance to the next person if possible.
2. Everyone puts on a blindfold and places his or hands out, palms up.
3. The group goal is to form a perfect square with a rope the facilitator will be giving you and using its entire length. Each side of the square must be equal to one-fourth of the rope's length. When the group has reached consensus that they have formed the square, everyone lays the rope down on the floor, removes their blindfold, and inspects the results.
4. In achieving the objective, the group must adhere to the following guidelines:
    a. Blindfolds may not be removed at any time.
    b. You must keep both hands on the rope and not let go.
    c. You may hold only one section of the rope.
    d. You may slide along the rope or let it slide through your hands as necessary to accomplish the objective.
5. The group has fifteen minutes to accomplish this objective.

After completing the activity, answer the following questions:

1. What did you notice about who took charge? Who helped make significant progress in the exercise? What kinds of things did people say? Were the comments mostly positive or negative? How did that affect the group?
2. What feelings did you experience during the activity?
3. Where did those feelings come from?
4. What group or individual behaviors contributed to your feelings?
5. What behaviors helped the group reach the objective?
6. What specific behaviors got in the way of the group's reaching its objective?
7. Do you ever see yourself doing these behaviors (either type)?
8. What lessons can you take away from this activity to reduce frustration or confusion and raise your group's performance level?

Activity 6.3

Movie Activity: *Freedom Writers*

The Five Practices of Exemplary Leadership show up in many movies. This activity features selected clips that illustrate the use of Enable Others to Act. Included is a brief synopsis of the film, a description of the clips that showcase the practice, and then a series of questions for you to answer or consider.

Movies are a great ways to spark your creative thinking about how The Five Practices show up in real life. While the clips listed here are clear examples of Enable Others to Act, look for examples of any of the other practices or leadership behaviors.

Movie

2007. Director: Richard LaGravenese

Screenplay: Richard LaGravenese

Distribution: Paramount Pictures

Rated PG-13 for violent content, some thematic material and language (none of the scenes for this activity include those elements).

Synopsis

This movie is based on the diaries written by students at Woodrow Wilson High School in Los Angeles. Teacher Erin Gruwell is in her first teaching job and works with at-risk students challenged by a community of violence, drugs, gangs, and little hope or promise to achieve anything beyond the life they know.

Scene Descriptions

The descriptions of two scenes in the film illustrate Enable Others to Act. You can view these scenes as individual clips, stopping to discuss them in between, or as a collective sequence with discussion afterward. In each scene, you will find examples that you can use to supplement the conversation about leadership and Enable Others to Act (as well as other practices).

Theme: Heroes. Begins in chapter 12 on the DVD at approximately 1:21:03 to 1:28:55.

This scene depicts an example of how relationships evolve and trust is built as people get closer to each other, in this case by finding experiences they can share. The students' inspiration comes from each other: after reading *The Diary of Anne Frank,* they believe that they can bring Meip Gies (the woman who helped hide Anne Frank from the Nazis in World War II) to speak at their school. They find within each other that they have the capacity to make this seemingly impossible visit happen. As they gain confidence in themselves, they develop a stronger belief that anything is possible if they are creative and persistent.

Theme: Courage. Begins in chapter 13 on the DVD at approximately 1:28:57 to 1:34:18.

This scene begins with two characters struggling to resolve difficult personal situations: Marcus, who has been estranged from his mother for years, and Eva who, in the finale to one of the film's substories, must testify in a murder trial involving a man from a street gang that her father (who is currently in jail) belongs to. Eva is being pressured because of her father's gang affiliation to testify that someone other than the accused actually committed the murder. Her honest testimony puts her and her family in danger of retaliation.

Leadership Lessons from Freedom Writers

Discussion Questions for "Heroes"

1. Describe the examples of Enable Others to Act you saw in "Heroes."
2. In the latter part of the scene, when Ms. Gies is speaking, how do her words show Enable Others to Act?

Discussion Question for "Courage"

1. What Enable Others to Act behaviors did you observe in "Courage"?

Discussion Question for Both Scenes

1. In either scene, what other practices or leadership behaviors did you notice?

CONNECT ENABLE OTHERS TO ACT TO MODULE 8: PERSONAL LEADERSHIP JOURNAL

The Personal Leadership Journal is available to help you shape your ongoing learning about each practice. There are three sections:

Section 1: Complete this section once you have had an opportunity to do a thorough review of your Student LPI report. You may be asked to complete this outside the classroom or formal workshop time, though that choice is up to your instructor. If you have not taken the Student LPI, complete this after you have a good understanding of Enable Others to Act and the behaviors aligned with that practice.

Section 2: Complete this section after you have taken action. It will help guide you on to your next targeted action step.

Section 3: Use this section as a support tool for your ongoing and independent exploration of Enable Others to Act.

MODULE 7

Encourage
the Heart

PRACTICE SUMMARY

Making extraordinary things happen in organizations is hard work. The climb to the summit is arduous and steep. Leaders encourage others to continue the quest. They expect the best of people and create self-fulfilling prophecies about how ordinary people can achieve extraordinary results. By maintaining a positive outlook and providing motivating feedback, leaders stimulate, focus, and rekindle people's energies and drive. These are all essentials to Encourage the Heart.

Leaders have high expectations of both themselves and of their constituents. They provide others with clear direction, substantial encouragement, personal attention, and meaningful feedback. They make people feel like winners, and winners like to continue raising the stakes.

Leaders give heart by visibly recognizing people's contributions to the common vision. They express pride in the accomplishments of their groups. They make others feel like heroes by telling the rest of the organization about what these individuals and the group have accomplished.

Celebrating group accomplishments adds fun to hard work and reinforces group spirit. Celebrations increase people's network of connections and promote information sharing. Fostering high-quality interpersonal relationships enhances productivity along with both physical and psychological health.

We highly recommend you read *The Student Leadership Challenge* book to deepen your understanding of The Five Practices of Exemplary Leadership model by reading about students who demonstrate the leadership behaviors embedded in the model. We learn from stories, and the stories in the book are intended to both inspire and delight you.

UNDERSTAND AND PRACTICE THE LEADERSHIP BEHAVIORS OF ENCOURAGE THE HEART

When I gave praise on people's work, they seemed to work harder because they were proud of the work that they had done.
—SHERI LEE

The following activities will help you explore and deepen your understanding of the leadership behaviors that connect to Encourage the Heart. Focus on one behavior at a time, and identify opportunities to demonstrate that behavior more often.

NOTE

For each behavior, you will find two iterations of the statement that describes the behavior: (1) the statement as it appears in the Student LPI and (2) the behavior as it is described in the student report that is generated from taking the Student LPI.

ENCOURAGE
THE HEART

"I encourage others as they work on activities and programs." (*Student LPI Report:* "Encourages others.")

1.   What are some of the ways you have encouraged others as they were doing something? What reactions did you get from them? Describe how that encouragement made a difference in the person, group, or outcome of the project—or all of these.

Describe a time when you have, at that very moment, recognized someone for what he or she was doing right then and there.

If so, what reaction did they have?

What impact do you think this action would have on the group and the individual if you did it more often?

2.   What are some simple ways you can acknowledge someone while he or she is in the middle of a project or assignment? What would you need to be looking for in order to recognize someone, and then how would you use what you have learned? Are there some experiences that you can learn from where you might have missed opportunities to recognize others?

List five simple, quick ways you could recognize someone for something he or she was doing in the group at that exact moment:

1.

2.

3.

4.

5.

Now that you have some ways in your mind to recognize someone as that person is working on something, what would you want to be looking for that you would feel is important to recognize? Can you list fifteen things?

1.

2.

3.

4.

5.

6.

7.

8.

9.

10.

11.

12.

13.

14.

15.

Have you seen anyone do any of the things you just mentioned? If so, did you recognize them? How did you do that? If not, what can you learn from those experiences so that you don't miss the opportunity again?

3. How do you think group members could be even more committed to the group than they already are? What are some things that you think would help some in the group to be more committed but others not as much?

If you were to regularly and sincerely recognize people in the group what overall outcome do you think that would have on the group as a whole?

What are the:

Benefits to the group for doing this?

Liabilities to the group for doing this?

"I express appreciation for the contributions people make." (*Student LPI Report:* "Expresses appreciation for people's contributions.")

1.   How can you show appreciation to your group for the various kinds of work that they do? Can you think of some of the more common ways to show appreciation to the group? Do you know specifically what expressing appreciation for their contributions means to those in the group? In other words, what expressions of appreciation do people in the group need that you can provide?

If you were asked what kind of appreciation the group needs to succeed, how would you answer?

How do you know what kind of appreciation the group would value (what the members need to be successful)? Explain:

List five things you can do to show greater appreciation to the group as a whole:

1.

2.

3.

4.

5.

If you showed appreciation for the group more often, how would individual members benefit?

How would the group benefit?

2. Share a few ways in which you have been showing appreciation to individual members in the group. If you can recall only a few instances of this, what can you specifically do to notice more individuals and what they are doing, and what can you do to take a moment to thank them?

List five of the really exciting ways that you have shown appreciation to someone in the group:

1.

2.

3.

4.

5.

If you could not name five, what could you do to take greater notice about what someone in the group is doing to make a difference?

3. Sometimes when groups are working on big projects, there can be a great sense of pressure or stress. These can be tremendous opportunities for you to learn what group members need. How could you take advantage of these opportunities to watch for and listen to what the members could use to help them carry on? What role would you see yourself in during these high-pressure times in terms of supporting others?

List some roles for pressure in a group doing its work and being successful:

Positive roles:

Negative roles:

What signs would you notice indicating that group members were feeling pressure?

Showing that you care about someone is a simple yet overlooked quality to the success of a leader.
—DAVID BRAVERMAN

What can you do as a leader to support and acknowledge others during these stressful periods?

ENCOURAGE THE HEART

"I make sure that people are creatively recognized for their contributions." (Student LPI Report: "Creatively recognizes people's contributions.")

1. Begin to keep a list or journal of various ways in which you could recognize someone. While this practice focuses on how the recognition needs to be personal to the individual being acknowledged, it can be helpful to have a tool like a journal or log in your smart phone to trigger some ideas for yourself when the time comes.

2. To make recognition personal, you need to know the people in the group. The majority of organizations that you are involved in won't be so large that you can't get to know everyone to some degree. Challenge yourself to reach out to those in the organization you might not know so well and get to know them better. In fact, identify three people in one of the groups you're in, and make a commitment to get to know him or her more personally over the next few days. Leaders who know their groups well will also be more aware of the things members are doing so they can be recognized.

List three people you will reach out to over the next three days and get to know more about them personally with the idea in mind that you want to learn what inspires and encourages them in their lives. List what you learned here.

Person	Personal Inspiration/Encouragement
1.	
2.	
3.	

By publicly praising people, you make a statement for how you wish other people, not directly involved in the praise, to work and act. Public, well-deserved, and fact-based appreciation can hence have a multiplier effect.

—KAJSA RYTTBERG

3. An easy way to keep track of what is important to people in a group is to keep a log of some sort. Just as you have a system for remembering phone numbers, birthdays, and e-mail addresses, you can keep notes, say in your smart phone, of things you want to remember about people—for example, favorite foods, sports teams, preferred colors, and music.

Create a template to use in your smart phone, computer, or other medium to know what information to collect about people in the group. This could be something as simple as the name and encouragement you learned about in the previous question. Or it could be more detailed so you know things like birthdays, favorite foods, colors, sports teams, or music. List the fields you want to log in for the people in the groups you lead or participate in.

ENCOURAGE
THE HEART

> "I praise people for a job well done." (*Student LPI Report:* "Praises people.")

1.   Name a time you were recognized for something you did. How did that feel? If you were to recognize someone else, would he or she feel the same way?

Remember a time (as recently as you can recall) when you were recognized in any way for something you did. Describe the feeling and reaction you had.

Describe how you did anything differently with that group after you were recognized.

How do you think others might feel the same or differently from the way you did?

2.   What do you think recognizing other people does for them? Why would praising someone for a job well done motivate, encourage, and engage that person? How does recognizing someone bear on his or her work and interactions in the group?

Describe the feelings or reactions you believe others have when they are recognized for something they have done.

How do you think the way they feel contributes to their work and interaction in the group?

Describe why recognizing someone matters.

3. Think of someone you have seen in the past week do something meaningful for a group you are in. Did you do anything to recognize that person? Why or why not? If not, how might you still recognize that person now?

In the past week did you recognize anyone for something that affected the group?
Circle one: Yes No

If so:
Why did you decide to do that?

What did you do, and why did you choose that approach?

If you didn't at the time:
Why not?

Could you recognize that person now? If so, how would you do it? What would it matter if you did a recognition now?

4. Make a list of twenty-five ways you could recognize someone for a contribution he or she might make. Don't consider what the recognition is or how practical it is. Just create the list. (We'll explore this again in another leadership behavior.)

Twenty-Five Ways to Recognize Someone for a Contribution

1.

2.

3.

4.

5.

6.

7.

8.

9.

10.

11.

12.

13.

14.

15.

16.

17.

18.

19.

20.

21.

22.

23.

24.

25.

"I make it a point to publicly recognize people who show commitment to shared values." (*Student LPI report:* "Publicly recognizes alignment with values.")

1.   As a leader, think about how the group's values look when they are being demonstrated or acted on. In other words, what is someone doing when he or she is demonstrating integrity (or whatever other values the group holds)? By reflecting on this, you know what to look for when people are demonstrating their commitment to the group's values.

Can you identify something in the recent past that someone in the group did that directly related to what the group holds as its highest values?

What was it that the person did?

What did you or the group do to acknowledge that person's actions?

If this person went unrecognized, what can you do the next time this opportunity arises?

2.   Once you know what aligning one's behavior with the group's values looks like, the next step is to recognize that. Think about the when, what, and why of the ways you can do that. Think about how you can recognize someone. When did the person do it? What specifically did he or she do? And why does it matter to the group? Think these questions through, and be prepared when the times arise for you to recognize others.

You might think of the example you gave in question 1 or another experience and describe the when, what, and why approach you followed to recognize someone.

When did the "thing" that someone did happen?

What did the person do?

Why does it matter to the group?

3.   There are many ways to recognize someone publicly. One thing to consider is how comfortable various individuals in the group are with different types of public recognition. Think about some of the ways you could recognize someone publicly so you have a good collection of ideas to match an appropriate method with people in the group.

Describe five ways that you can publicly recognize someone for something he or she contributed. Try to come up with ways you can do this beyond the traditional recognition dinners, social hours, or regular group meetings:

1.

2.

3.

4.

5.

ENCOURAGE
THE HEART

"I find ways for us to celebrate accomplishments." (*Student LPI Report:* "Celebrates accomplishments.")

1. Think about all kinds of ways that you could celebrate accomplishments of the group. Remember that this behavior focuses on "us," as in "the group as a whole." Describe five ways that you can publicly recognize the entire group for something they contributed. Try to come up with ways you can do this beyond the traditional recognition dinners, social hours, or regular group meetings:

1.

2.

3.

4.

5.

2. Think about how you can make various recognitions for the group in a public manner. There might be an occasion to recognize a committee within the group or the group as a whole. How can you let others know about the group's accomplishments in a way that recognizes the contribution the group makes, say, to the campus, school, or organization as a whole?

Describe five ways that you can let others throughout the school or organization and community know about something the group accomplished:

1.

2.

3.

4.

5.

FURTHER ACTIONS TO IMPROVE IN ENCOURAGE THE HEART

A list of suggested actions follows that you can try in order to Encourage the Heart more often. Some of the specific leadership behaviors in the Student LPI that are influenced by these actions are listed by number following each suggestion (see Appendix A for the complete list of Student LPI statements and behaviors).

1. If your group is working on a larger project or event, identify small milestones along the way that would be appropriate places for you to celebrate. Don't wait until the

entire project is finished. Celebrating your success and progress along the way will encourage others to keep going. (10, 25)

2. As often as you can, share a story publicly with the group or other appropriate audience about someone in the group who did something exceptional—that is, that person went above and beyond the call of duty. (5, 10, 15, 20, 30)

3. When recognizing someone, think of the three Ws: who, what, and why. Recognize the person by name (*who*). Describe *what* the person did. You don't need to go into immense detail, but share enough of the story so others can see how exceptional the work was. Finally, tell *why* what the person did mattered to the group. Connect this person's work to the values of the organization to demonstrate that you recognize how he or she is truly making a difference to make the group better. (5, 20, 30)

4. Use informal times and gatherings to find out what others are doing that exemplify what the group stands for. Take a moment to recognize these people on the spot. (10, 20, 30)

5. When you talk with someone in the group and get to know him or her, find out what encourages this person. Ask how he or she likes to be recognized and what has meaning for him or her. You might ask about times in the past when something special was done for that person and what that meant. When the time comes, you will be prepared to recognize this person in a meaningful way. (5, 10, 15, 30)

6. Write at least three thank-you notes every week to those who are doing work that supports and improves the group. (5, 15, 30)

7. If you receive or hear acknowledgments of good work from others about people in your group, be sure to pass those comments along to that person in a public way. You might read the note aloud at a meeting, put it on your group's website, or release it through social media. (5, 20, 25, 30)

8. Be on the lookout for creative gifts you can use to recognize and reward people. You can find inexpensive items in retail stores that you can easily relate a story to. You can also use things you might come across, such as photos, buttons, small stuffed animals, painted rocks, ribbons, or some other trinkets. It is not the gift but the thought and the story that goes with the gift that matters the most. (5, 10, 15, 30)

9. Create some tools anyone in the group can use to recognize others at any time. Preprint some note cards or pads, for example, or come up with a unique award or something that you can turn into a tradition for the group when others want to acknowledge exceptional work. (25, 30)

10. If you do have end-of-term or end-of-school-year activities, go beyond the typical certificate or plaques and be sure to put personal stories behind the recognition. If someone has been doing extraordinary work and made an important impact on the group, acknowledge those contributions by sharing them with the audience. You will give greater meaning to the contributions by sharing a personal story about the individual. (5, 15, 20, 25, 30)

ACTIVITIES TO LEARN ABOUT AND APPLY ENCOURAGE THE HEART

Activity 7.1

Web of Appreciation

Overview

This activity helps you acknowledge others and creates a visual metaphor for the connection and unity of the group.

Objectives

After completing the exercise, you will be able to:

- Acknowledge each member of the group for a specific contribution and identify how it contributed
- Build a physical web of yarn that represents the interconnectedness of the group
- Acknowledge that the more people rely on each other, the tighter and stronger the web becomes

Process

1. Form a circle. Your instructor will be in the middle of the circle and toss the ball of yarn he or she is holding to someone in the group.
2. This person unwinds several yards of the string or yarn in preparation for throwing it to someone else in the group.
3. Now identify a person you want to acknowledge. Name that person and say what he or she did that you want to acknowledge and why it mattered to you and to the rest of the group. Unwind several yards of the string or yarn, hold it tight at that point, and then toss the ball of yarn gently to that person.
4. That person repeats the process until everyone has a connection point with the yarn.

Activity 7.2

Recognition Cards

Overview

This activity is an opportunity for anyone to easily and quickly recognize and show appreciation to someone right on the spot.

Objectives

After completing the activity, you will be able to:

- Develop the ability to regularly look for ways in which others exemplify the organization's standards.
- Experience giving recognition as you see someone doing something that improves the group or shows commitment to the group's values—or both.

Process

1. Your instructor will give you a supply of Encourage the Heart recognition cards (Figure 7.1) or you can create some yourself. Fill out a recognition card whenever you see a group member (or any other student, for that matter) doing something that you believe exemplifies the standards of the organization, demonstrates the values of the organization, works to go above and beyond typical actions, provides a great idea, supports another member or helps them in some way become successful, or something else.
2. Be specific about what the person did and what impact he or she had.
3. When you give out the cards, consider the impact you are having on the other person. What do you think he or she is thinking and feeling? How do you believe this sense of appreciation will affect the work he or she is doing? What would happen if you did something like this to group members on a regular basis?

Figure 7.1 Sample Encourage the Heart Card

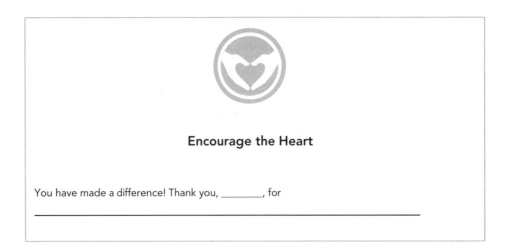

Activity 7.3

Movie Activity: *Harry Potter and the Sorcerer's Stone*

The Five Practices of Exemplary Leadership show up in many movies. This activity features a selected clip that illustrates the use of Encourage the Heart. Included is a brief synopsis of the film, a description of the clips that showcase this practice, followed by a series of questions for you to answer or consider.

Movies are a great ways to spark your creative thinking about how the Five Practices show up in real life. While the clip listed here is a clear example of Encourage the Heart, look for examples of any of the other practices or leadership behaviors.

Movie

2002. Director: Chris Columbus
Screenplay: Steve Kloves
Distribution: Warner Bros. Pictures
Rated PG for some intense moments and mild language (the scene for this activity does
    not include those elements)

This movie is based on the book written by J. K. Rowling about a boy who attends a school for wizardry. Harry Potter spends his first year of school challenged with fighting for good and against evil.

Synopsis

Harry Potter, a first-year student at Hogwarts School of Witchcraft and Wizardry, is a member of one of four residential houses at Hogwarts that typically are in competition with each other in a number of sports and academic contexts. Harry makes close friends with many of the students, and his family history of wizardry makes him popular throughout the school. Still, some in the school despise him and create difficult and dangerous situations for Harry and his friends to face throughout the film. They all survive their first year relatively unscathed.

Scene Description

The following scene in the film offers examples that you can use to supplement the conversation about leadership and Encourage the Heart (as well as other practices).

Theme: House Cup Winner. Begins in chapter 33 of the DVD at approximately 2:17:44 to
    2:21:35.

Professor Albus Dumbledore, the headmaster of Hogwarts, is winding down the
    school year and awarding the house cup to one of four residential houses based on

a series of competitive events and other contributions to the school. In announcing the winner of the year's house cup, the professor describes a number of actions that members of one house took throughout the movie.

Leadership Lessons from *Harry Potter and the Sorcerer's Stone*
Discussion Questions for "House Cup Winner"

1. What examples of Encourage the Heart did you see in this scene?
2. What things did the headmaster say in his remarks that makes this an example of Encourage the Heart? Is there anything he might have done differently?
3. Was there anything different about how the headmaster recognized each person?
4. After the remarks, did you notice anything happening with everyone in the banquet hall?

CONNECT ENCOURAGE THE HEART TO MODULE 8: PERSONAL LEADERSHIP JOURNAL

The Personal Leadership Journal is available to help you shape your ongoing learning about each practice. There are three sections:

Section 1: Complete this section once you have had an opportunity to do a thorough review of your Student LPI report. You may be asked to complete this outside the classroom or formal workshop time, though that choice is up to your instructor. If you have not taken the Student LPI, complete this after you have a good understanding of Encourage the Heart and the behaviors aligned with that practice.

Section 2: Complete this section after you have taken action. It will help guide you on to your next targeted action step.

Section 3: Use this section as a support tool for your ongoing and independent exploration of Encourage the Heart.

Personal Leadership Journal

OVERVIEW AND GUIDELINES FOR CONTINUING YOUR LEADERSHIP DEVELOPMENT JOURNEY

Your leadership development begins when you answer the call to accept personal responsibility to develop the leader within you. But it doesn't end there. The Leadership Challenge research tells us that this will be an ongoing process, one that requires deliberate and reiterative practice. That practice is most effective when you take some time to reflect on what you've learned along the way. That continued learning, beyond a workshop or a class, plays a key role in your ability to liberate the leader within. This Personal Leadership Journal is intended to support your ongoing leadership journey.

Each section of the journal is linked to one of The Five Practices of Exemplary Leadership and builds on your Student LPI feedback. The sections are organized into three parts: (1) Take Action, (2) Look Within, and (3) Ongoing Learning. Here's what you'll do in each of these.

Take Action (What Do You Intend to Do?)

There is no substitute for learning by doing. The Student LPI data indicate that the more frequently you can demonstrate the essential leadership behaviors, the greater the possibility is that you will lead others to achieve extraordinary results. It is in the doing that you discover your potential to engage others in meaningful change. Use the journal to define the actions you will take.

Changing your behavior in any way can be a challenge, and taking small steps is one of the best ways to meet the challenge. For example, a soccer player who wants to improve her game might take time to focus on one skill. Perhaps one day's practice is on building speed and another day on agility with the ball. Practicing the individual parts gives the player an immediate goal that aligns with the long-range goal of being a stronger player. The same applies here: find ways to demonstrate and practice the behaviors that will strengthen your leadership capacity. Every goal for tomorrow requires some action today.

A good way to identify those small steps is by committing to S.M.A.R.T. actions. This acronym stands for: **S**pecific, **M**easurable, **A**ttainable, **R**ealistic, **T**imely. Identifying S.M.A.R.T. actions can greatly increase the likelihood that you will keep your commitment.

Look Within (What Did You Learn from Taking Action?)

As you practice, take some time to reflect on what you are learning. Lessons are always available if you take the time to look within and listen. Get in the habit of taking a few moments of quiet time each day to answer the questions here. Note what you learn about yourself and from others. Find ways to apply that in the days ahead.

Ongoing Learning (What Will You Do Next Based upon This Experience?)

In the practice modules in this workbook, we offered you some suggestions for actions to take to work on each leadership practice. The "Ongoing Learning" sections throughout this Personal Leadership Journal ask you to choose one of these suggestions and commit to it as a way to deepen your practice of the behaviors and refine your philosophy of leadership.

AFTER REVIEWING YOUR STUDENT LPI DATA

Take Action (What Do You Intend to Do?)

1. The leadership practices or behaviors I will focus on are:

2. Areas in my life where I will look for opportunities to take action:

Look Within (What Did You Learn from Taking Action?)

1. One way to build your commitment to leadership is to imagine the legacy you might leave down the road. Take time to reflect on and answer this question based on your current thinking.

I want to be known as a person who:

I want to be remembered as a leader who:

Ongoing Leadership Learning (What Will You Do Next Based on This Experience?)

1.   Review your Student LPI report, and note which practice you do the most frequently. What opportunities do you see to continue demonstrating that practice in the next week or two?

2.   Review the thirty leadership behaviors that make up your Student LPI report, and note any that you want to understand more fully. What questions do you have about them?

AFTER REVIEWING THE LEADERSHIP PRACTICE OF MODEL THE WAY

Take Action (What Do You Intend to Do?)

Use your Student LPI report and what you have learned about Model the Way to take action based on one of the six behaviors associated with this practice.

The leadership behavior I've chosen:

Your Actions

1. To demonstrate this behavior, the actions I need to take are:

2. Detail how each element of a S.M.A.R.T. action is addressed in your action plan.

Specific: Is your action clear and simple? Does it answer the following questions?

What do you want to accomplish?

Who is involved?

When will it take place?

Where will it take place?

Measurable: Is there a clear way to measure completion or success?

Attainable/Action-Oriented: Can this goal be accomplished? How?

Relevant/Reasonable: Is this action relevant for the goal you have in mind as a leader? How?

Timely: Is a time frame attached? If so, what is it?

Look Within (What Did You Learn from Taking Action?)

1. What happened when you took this action?

2. What were the results of taking this action?

3. What did you learn about the value of demonstrating this leadership behavior?

4. What parts of this action were comfortable and easy? What was difficult? What might your answers tell you about yourself as a leader?

Ongoing Learning (What Will You Do Next Based on This Experience?)

Refine your philosophy of leadership. With deeper understanding of Model the Way, is there anything you would like to add or revise in your answer to the question, "I want to be known as a leader who _____"?

Commit to deepening your practice. Following are examples of things you can do to Model the Way that were suggested in Module 3. Review them, pick one from the list to commit to, or identify another way to practice Model the Way, and then describe what you will do to meet that commitment.

1. At the beginning of each day, reflect on what you want to achieve for that day. Think in terms of what you know is important to you and what in your schedule contributes to that importance. You might ask yourself, "How do I want to show up as a leader today?" At the end of the day, reflect on what happened. What did you do as a leader that you are most proud of? Where were the opportunities that you missed that you could take advantage of another day? Can you do anything tomorrow about those opportunities? What other actions can you take tomorrow to enable you to lead better? (1, 26)

2. If you are in a group and have a formal, defined leadership role, see how you can work directly with or shadow someone else in the group. In essence, trade places with that person and work on something together. Use this as an opportunity to get feedback from others as to what you are doing related to their work in the group. (6, 16)

3. Use a planner, smart phone, journal, note app, or some other resource you use regularly to write notes to yourself about the commitments and promises you are making to yourself and others. Write the dates you have committed to fulfilling them, and check regularly on your progress. (1, 11, 26)

4. Focus on the little things that your groups or the people you lead are doing. You can become easily engaged in the larger projects or tasks, but remember that it is the smaller details together that help others (and the projects) achieve success. Without micromanaging, look for places where you can make a difference. Think about how you use the smaller things that need attention to reinforce what you and the organization stand for. (1, 6, 16, 21, 26)

5. Keep track of how you spend your time. What is important to you and what you value often show up in how you spend your time and prioritize what you do each day and over the course of weeks and months. Look to see if you are investing large amounts of your time in things that are not that important to you or that you don't value. The same might also be said about people and relationships. What can you do to adjust your schedule so that you are aligning your actions more with your values? (1, 6, 11, 21, 26)

6. If you are in an organized student group, visit other teams or groups at your school that are similar and even different from yours that you know are considered really strong groups. Talk to their leaders, and ask what they are doing that could give you greater insight in to leading. You don't have to be talking about doing exactly the same things to learn and get feedback from how others lead and work. Learn what makes the other group so successful. (16, 21, 26)

7. Study other leaders and organizations that you think live out their ideas and values as a group. These could be groups that you identified in the previous item, or groups, organizations, or companies that are known to have strong values and demonstrate those values in their daily work. (1, 2, 16, 21)

Ways that I will practice Model the Way and how I will do that:

AFTER REVIEWING THE LEADERSHIP PRACTICE OF INSPIRE A SHARED VISION

Take Action (What Do You Intend to Do?)

Use your Student LPI report and what you have learned about Inspire a Shared Vision to take action based on one of the six behaviors associated with this practice.

The leadership behavior I've chosen:

Your Actions

    1.   To demonstrate this behavior from Inspire a Shared Vision, the actions I need to take are:

    2.   Detail how each element of a S.M.A.R.T. action is addressed in your action plan. *Specific:* Is your action clear and simple? Does it answer the following questions?

    What do you want to accomplish?

    Who is involved?

    When will it take place?

    Where will it take place?

Measurable: Is there a clear way to measure completion or success?

Attainable/Action-Oriented: Can this goal be accomplished? How?

Relevant/Reasonable: Is this action relevant for the goal you have in mind as a leader? How?

Timely: Is a time frame attached? If so, what is it?

Look Within (What Did You Learn from Taking Action?)

1. What happened when you took this action?

2. What were the results of taking this action?

3. What did you learn about the value of demonstrating this behavior?

4. What parts of this action were comfortable and easy? What was difficult? What might your answers tell you about yourself as a leader?

Ongoing Learning (What Will You Do Next Based on This Experience?)

Refine your philosophy of leadership. With deeper understanding of Inspire a Shared Vision, is there anything you would like to add or revise in your answer to the question, "I want to be known as a leader who _____"?

Commit to deepening your practice. Following are examples of things you can do to Inspire a Shared Vision that were suggested in module 4. Review them, pick one from the list to commit to, or define another way to practice Inspire a Shared Vision, and then describe what you will do to meet that commitment.

1. Talk with an advisor, coach, or staff member or teacher about how you might think of some new ways in which you can help a group look at its vision more clearly and about different ways in which the group might better align with its vision. (2, 12, 22, 27)

2. Take stock of what you get excited about with your group. How does that excitement influence what you can do to connect with others in the group? What conversations will help others see the possibilities you can explore together to better realize your vision? (7, 12, 22, 27)

3. Imagine that it's one year from today: What is different about the group? What has it accomplished? How is the group better off than it was a year ago? Why? (2, 7, 12)

4. Talk with individuals in your group about their hopes and aspirations for the organization. Figure out what is shared and how those things relate to what you personally envision for the group. Think about how the group's vision is or is not in alignment with what others in the group think. (7, 12, 17)

5. The next several times you meet or talk with people in your group gatherings, listen for the language they use. Is it tentative or noncommittal, such as, "We'll try," or, "We could/should"? Can you make sure that it is more positive and committed, such as, "We will!"? (7, 22, 27)

6. As a leader, ask yourself, "Am I in this role because of something I can or want to accomplish for myself?" or, "Am I here to do something for others?" Are you working to lead the group toward the group's shared vision or your own agenda? (12, 17, 27)

7. Sharing a vision requires clarity and confidence. If it is difficult for you to talk emphatically and confidently to a group, look for multiple opportunities, such as other student groups that involve public speaking, to speak in front of people no matter what the purpose. The more often you do this, the more confident and comfortable you will be in speaking situations. (22, 27)

8. Who are other leaders you find inspiring? Read about them to see how they communicate their vision for those they lead. What is it about what and how they say things that stand out to you and cause the reason for your inspiration? Think about how you can learn from what they say and do. (2, 12, 22, 27)

Ways that I will practice Inspire a Shared Vision and how I will do that:

AFTER REVIEWING THE LEADERSHIP PRACTICE OF CHALLENGE THE PROCESS

Take Action (What Do You Intend to Do?):

Use your Student LPI report and what you have learned about Challenge the Process to take action based on one of the six behaviors associated with this practice.

The leadership behavior I've chosen:

Your Actions

1. To demonstrate this behavior from Challenge the Process, the actions I need to take are:

2. Detail how each element of a S.M.A.R.T. action is addressed in your action plan.

Specific: Is your action clear and simple? Does it answer the questions?

What do you want to accomplish?

Who is involved?

When will it take place?

Where will it take place?

Measurable: Is there a clear way to measure completion or success?

Attainable/Action-Oriented: Can this goal be accomplished? How?

Relevant/Reasonable: Is this action relevant for the goal you have in mind as a leader? How?

Timely: Is a time frame attached? If so, what is it?

Look Within (What Did You Learn from Taking Action?)

1. What happened when you took this action?

2. What were the results of taking this action?

3. What did you learn about the value of demonstrating this behavior?

4. What parts of this action were comfortable and easy? What was difficult? What might your answers tell you about yourself as a leader?

Ongoing Learning (What Will You Do Next Based on This Experience?)

Refine your philosophy of leadership. With deeper understanding of Challenge the Process, is there anything you would like to add or revise in your answer to the question "I want to be known as a leader who_____"?

Commit to deepening your practice. Following are examples of things you can do to Challenge the Process that were suggested in module 5. Review them, pick one from the list to commit to, or define another way to practice Inspire a Shared Vision, and then describe what you will do to meet that commitment.

1. Make a list of tasks that you perform that are related to your various leadership activities. For each task, ask yourself, "Why am I doing this? Why am I doing it this way? Can this task be eliminated or done significantly better?" Based on your responses, do you see where you can develop other skills? Identify those skills and look for applicable opportunities within your leadership activities where you can work to develop the skills you have identified. (3, 8)

2. Make a list of the things your group does that are basically done the same way as they have always been done before. For each routine, ask, "Are we doing this at our best?" If yes, then carry on! If no, look for ways to change to make it better. (8, 18, 28)

3. Continue to observe and learn about what makes other leaders successful, and then think about your own skills. Which skills do you see those leaders having that you don't have? Perhaps you believe you have those skills but need to strengthen them. Talk to those individuals and ask for their suggestions on what you could do to get stronger. If you don't have that opportunity, write down the skills or abilities you want to work on and ask an advisor, teacher, coach, or student life staff member to help you find places at your school or organization where you can develop those skills. (3, 13)

4. Ask others in your group what frustrates them about the organization. Make a commitment to change three of the most frequently mentioned items that are frustrating people and probably hindering the group's success. (13, 18)

5. Identify a process in your group that's not working, and take action to fix it. Learn from your experience. (18, 28)

6. Experiment by doing something you are not currently doing that will benefit your group—perhaps something new you can do within a project or event you are already working on. You might find something new you can do together that can meet a goal of your group. Make your experiments small, and learn from them for future larger experiments. (8, 28)

7. Eliminate "fire hosing" (throwing water on every new idea without giving it consideration). Remove from your group's vocabulary the "That'll never work" phrase or "The problem with that is . . ." At the very least, give new ideas the benefit of discussion and reflection. Recognize that even if the first idea isn't valuable, it might lead to others that are. (8, 18, 28)

8. Call or visit your counterparts in other organizations at your school, another school or group, or another community (both those in groups similar to yours and different from yours). Find out what they are doing and learn from their successes and challenges. Copy what they do well and use their failures as a guide for improvement. (13)

9. Set achievable goals. Tell people what the key milestones are and review them frequently so that you and they can easily see progress. (23)

10. Eliminate the phrase, "That's the way we did it last year," from all discussions. Use the results of past programs or projects to learn from, but don't fall into the trap of doing something the same way simply because it's easier. (8, 23, 28)

Ways that I will practice Challenge the Process and how I will do that:

AFTER REVIEWING THE LEADERSHIP PRACTICE OF ENABLE OTHERS TO ACT

Take Action (What Do You Intend to Do?)

Use your Student LPI report and what you have learned about Enable Others to Act to take action based on one of the six behaviors associated with this practice.

The leadership behavior I've chosen:

Your Actions

1. To demonstrate this behavior from Enable Others to Act, the actions I need to take are:

2. Detail how each element of a S.M.A.R.T. action is addressed in your action plan.

Specific: Is your action clear and simple? Does it answer the questions?

What do you want to accomplish?

Who is involved?

When will it take place?

Where will it take place?

Measurable: Is there a clear way to measure completion or success?

Attainable/Action-Oriented: Can this goal be accomplished? How?

Relevant/Reasonable: Is this action relevant for the goal you have in mind as a leader? How?

Timely: Is a time frame attached? If so, what is it?

Look Within (What Did You Learn from Taking Action?)

1. What happened when you took this action?

2. What were the results of taking this action?

3. What did you learn about the value of demonstrating this behavior?

4.   What parts of this action were comfortable and easy? What was difficult? What might your answers tell you about yourself as a leader?

Ongoing Learning (What Will You Do Next Based on This Experience?)

Refine your philosophy of leadership. With a deeper understanding of Enable Others to Act, is there anything you would like to add or revise in your answer to the question, "I want to be known as a leader who _____"?

Commit to deepening your practice. Following are examples of things you can do to Enable Others to Act that were suggested in module 5. Review them, pick one from the list to commit to, or define another way to practice Enable Others to Act, and then describe what you will do to meet that commitment.

1.   Teach others in your group to become leaders. Leaders bring others along to be leaders. Take some specific steps, perhaps starting with just one or two people, to help them develop their leadership abilities. (24, 29)

2.   Make a point of encouraging others to take on important tasks or projects. Put the names forward of people in the group you believe would be well suited for a certain project. Similarly, talk with them about taking on a responsibility on behalf of the group, letting them know that you have confidence in their ability and judgment. (4, 14, 19, 24, 29)

3.   Take another approach to item 2 by asking someone else to lead a group meeting or do a presentation so he or she can gain that experience (or any other experiences you identify). Then coach this person along the way to assist and support him or her in this new capacity. (4, 14, 24, 29)

4. Give something up altogether that you do on a regular basis. Don't just give up something you don't want to do, but find someone in the group you think would grow from taking over this task as a regular responsibility. Be sure to let him or her know that you are not just getting rid of something you no longer care to do or think is critical; rather, explain how this represents an opportunity for this person to grow and develop. (4, 9, 19, 24, 29)

5. Identify someone at your school or in your community who is known as an exceptional leader. Contact that person and find out if you can follow or shadow him or her for a few hours to learn about how you can become better in working with others. (4, 9, 14)

6. Improve relationships and develop a greater sense of trust with group members by doing something together outside regular group activities. Find ways to interact informally so you and they can build stronger bonds with each other. (4, 9, 14)

7. For the next two weeks, see how often you can replace "I" with "we" as you lead a group. Work to develop the philosophy and understanding that leadership is about the group or the team, not one individual. Every time you think about saying "I'm going to . . . ," say instead, "We can do this . . . " (4, 9, 14, 29)

8. Ask an athletic coach if you can watch a practice or team meeting to see how he or she helps athletes develop new skills or identify and reach new goals. Think about how you can apply these lessons to the groups to which you belong. (4, 9)

One way that I will practice Enable Others to Act and how I will do that:

AFTER REVIEWING THE LEADERSHIP PRACTICE OF ENCOURAGE THE HEART

Take Action (What Do You Intend to Do?):

Use your Student LPI report and what you have learned about Encourage the Heart to take action based on one of the six behaviors associated with this practice.
The leadership behavior I've chosen:

Your Actions

1. To demonstrate this behavior from Encourage the Heart, the actions I need to take are:

2. Detail how each element of a S.M.A.R.T. action is addressed in your action plan.
Specific: Is your action clear and simple? Does it answer the questions?
What do you want to accomplish?

Who is involved?

When will it take place?

Where will it take place?

Measurable: Is there a clear way to measure completion or success?

Attainable/Action-Oriented: Can this goal be accomplished? How?

Relevant/Reasonable: Is this action relevant for the goal you have in mind as a leader? How?

Timely: Is a time frame attached? If so, what is it?

Look Within (What Did You Learn from Taking Action?)

1. What happened when you took this action?

2. What were the results of taking this action?

3. What did you learn about the value of demonstrating this behavior?

4. What parts of this action were comfortable and easy? What was difficult? What might your answers tell you about yourself as a leader?

Ongoing Learning (What Will You Do Next Based on This Experience?)

Refine your philosophy of leadership. With a deeper understanding of Encourage the Heart, is there anything you would like to add or revise in your answer to the question, "I want to be known as a leader who _____"?

Commit to deepening your practice. Following are examples of things you can do to Encourage the Heart that were suggested in module 7. Review them, pick one from the list to commit to, or define another way to practice Encourage the Heart, and then describe what you will do to meet that commitment.

1. If your group is working on a larger project or event, identify small milestones along the way that would be appropriate places for you to celebrate. Don't wait until the entire project is finished. Celebrating your success and progress along the way will encourage others to keep going. (10, 25)

2. As often as you can, share a story publicly with the group or other appropriate audiences about someone in the group who did something exceptional; that is, that person went above and beyond the call of duty. (5, 10, 15, 20, 30)

3. When recognizing someone, think of the "three Ws": who, what, and why. Recognize the person by name (*who*). Describe *what* the person did. You don't need to go into immense detail, but share enough of the story so others can see how exceptional the work was. Finally, tell *why* what the person did mattered to the group. Connect this person's work to the values of the organization to demonstrate that you recognize how he or she is truly making a difference to make the group better. (5, 20, 30)

4. Use informal times and gatherings to find out what others are doing that exemplify what the group stands for. Take a moment to recognize these people on the spot. (10, 20, 30)

5. When you talk with someone in the group and are getting to know him or her, find out what encourages this person. Ask how he or she likes to be recognized and what has meaning for him or her. You might ask about times in the past when something special was done for that person and what that meant. When the time comes, you will be prepared to recognize this person in a meaningful way. (5, 10, 15, 30)

6. Write at least three thank-you notes every week to those who are doing work (taking actions) that supports and improves the group. (5, 15, 30)

7. If you receive or hear acknowledgments of good work from others about people in your group, be sure to pass those comments along to them in a public way. You might read the note aloud at a meeting, put it on your group's website, or release it through social media. (5, 20, 25, 30)

8. Be on the lookout for creative gifts you can use to recognize and reward people. You can find inexpensive things in retail stores that you can easily relate a story to. You can also use things you might come across, such as photos, buttons, small stuffed animals, painted rocks, ribbons, or some other trinkets. It is not the gift but the thought and the story that goes with the gift that matter the most. (5, 10, 15, 30)

9. Create some tools anyone in the group can use to recognize others at any time. Preprint some note cards or pads, for example, or come up with a unique award or something that you can turn into a tradition for the group that others can give to someone doing exceptional work. (25, 30)

10. If you do have end-of-term or end-of-school-year activities, go beyond the typical certificate or plaque and be sure to put personal stories behind the recognition. If someone has been doing extraordinary work and really made an impact on the group, acknowledge those contributions by sharing them with the audience. You give greater meaning to the contributions by sharing an individual story about the individual. (5, 15, 20, 25, 30)

Ways that I will practice Encourage the Heart and how I will do that:

ONWARD!

Congratulations for navigating your way through this workbook! However far you made it through the many suggestions, activities, and reflections in it, you should feel great about yourself. We've tried to make leadership simple to understand and shown what it looks like in practice, but simple doesn't mean that it is easy to be a leader or to learn how to become an even better leader.

No one is perfect. Every leader has flaws, and no one gets it right the first time or even every time. In sports, we see how professionals make the difficult look easy and how amateurs make the easy look difficult. Being professional is an ongoing endeavor no matter the sport, the setting, or the situation. Being a leader is no different. Despite your best efforts and most noble intentions, things won't always work out as you hoped, people will not always do what they promised or are capable of, and forces beyond your control will derail your plans.

Perhaps the truest test of leadership is in people's ability to bounce back from defeat and adversity, to pick themselves up and try again. History shows us that this quality of resilience is characteristic of all great leaders, and deeper analyses show that this stems from their being both clear and committed to a set of values and way of being. Becoming a better leader, as we indicated at the onset, begins with clarifying your values, finding your voice, and conscientiously aligning your actions with shared values.

We first talked about leadership with Melissa Poe when she was nine years old. Melissa was concerned about the environment, and as she took action at that young age and heard from other kids who were as concerned as she was, she started a club for kids and by kids. Starting with just six members at her elementary school, Kids F.A.C.E. (for a clean environment) grew to more than 2,000 club chapters in twenty-two countries and more than 350,000 members during the time Melissa was president. (Today there are 500,000 members.) At age seventeen, she stepped aside, joined the board, and handed over the reins to two fifteen year olds, saying she was too old for the job. She wanted the organization to always be in kids' hands.

When we caught up with Melissa almost twenty-five years later, she told us, "I believe everyone struggles with life purpose; however, a leader is one who steps beyond her own self-doubts and realizes her journey is her responsibility. Whether one is a child or an adult, an individual participates in the world, and she should do so deliberately. Ultimately the worst thing one can do is to see a problem and think it is someone else's responsibility."

Melissa reminds us that leadership is not about wishful thinking. It's about determined doing. There are no shortages of problems and opportunities at school, at home, in our neighborhoods, at work, and around the globe. There are no shortages of problems to solve. Leadership is not about telling others that they ought to solve these problems. It's about seeing a problem and accepting personal responsibility for doing something about it. And it's about holding yourself accountable for the actions that you take. The next time you see a problem and say, "Why doesn't someone do something about this?" take a look in the mirror and say instead, "I'll be the someone to do something about it."

This doesn't mean that you have to accept responsibility for every problem, and it doesn't mean that you should solve problems you see by yourself. What it does mean is that leaders are active participants who work tirelessly to mobilize others to want to work for shared aspirations. They are not bystanders in the parade of life. Leaders believe that they have an obligation to do something to bring about change and that they can move things forward with the active engagement of others.

You make a difference. Don't let anyone or anything that happens persuade you otherwise. You'll be amazed by how many opportunities you have every day to act as a leader and make a difference. And you'll be pleasantly surprised by how much improvement you will be able to make by being more conscientious and intentional about acting as a leader.

APPENDIX A

Student Leadership Practices Inventory Behavior Statements

Here are the six behavior statements from the Student Leadership Practices Inventory products for each of The Five Practices of Exemplary Leadership. The first iteration of the statement is the exact behavior. The iteration in parentheses is the way the behavior statement appears in the individual reports for the Student LPI 360 and Student LPI Self Online.

Model the Way Statements

1 "I set a personal example of what I expect from other people." ("Sets personal example.")

6 "I spend time making sure that people behave consistently with the principles and standards we have agreed on." ("Aligns others with principles and standards.")

11 "I follow through on the promises and commitments I make." ("Follows through on promises.")

16 "I seek to understand how my actions affect other people's performance." ("Seeks feedback about impact of actions.")

21 "I make sure that people support the values we have agreed upon." ("Makes sure people support common values.")

26 "I talk about my values and the principles that guide my actions." ("Talks about values and principles.")

Inspire a Shared Vision Statements

2 "I look ahead and communicate what I believe will affect us in the future." ("Looks ahead and communicates future.")

7 "I describe to others in our organization what we should be capable of accomplishing." ("Describes ideal capabilities.")

12 "I talk with others about a vision of how things could be even better in the future." ("Talks about how future could be better.")

17 "I talk with others about how their own interests can be met by working toward a common goal." ("Shows others how their interests can be realized.")

22 "I am upbeat and positive when talking about what we can accomplish." ("Is upbeat and positive.")

27 "I speak with passion about the higher purpose and meaning of what we are doing." ("Communicates purpose and meaning.")

Challenge the Process Statements

3 "I look for ways to develop and challenge my skills and abilities." ("Challenges skills and abilities.")

8 "I look for ways that others can try out new ideas and methods." ("Helps others try out new ideas.")

13 "I search for innovative ways to improve what we are doing." ("Searches for innovative ways to improve.")

18 "When things don't go as we expected, I ask, 'What can we learn from this experience?'" ("Asks, 'What can we learn?'")

23 "I make sure that big projects we undertake are broken down into smaller and doable parts." ("Breaks projects into smaller doable portions.")

28 "I take initiative in experimenting with the way things can be done." ("Takes initiative in experimenting.")

Enable Others to Act Statements

4 "I foster cooperative rather than competitive relationships among people I work with." ("Fosters cooperative relationships.")

9 "I actively listen to diverse points of view." ("Actively listens to diverse viewpoints.")

14 "I treat others with dignity and respect." ("Treats others with respect.")

19 "I support the decisions that other people make on their own." ("Supports decisions other people make.")

24 "I give others a great deal of freedom and choice in deciding how to do their work." ("Gives people choice about how to do their work.")

29 "I provide opportunities for others to take on leadership responsibilities." ("Provides leadership opportunities for others.")

Encourage the Heart Statements

5 "I praise people for a job well done." ("Praises people.")

10 "I encourage others as they work on activities and programs." ("Encourages others.")

15 "I express appreciation for the contributions that people make." ("Expresses appreciation for people's contributions.")

20 "I make it a point to publicly recognize people who show commitment to shared values." ("Publicly recognizes alignment with values.")

25 "I find ways for us to celebrate accomplishments." ("Celebrates accomplishments.")

30 "I make sure that people are creatively recognized for their contributions." ("Creatively recognizes people's contributions.")

APPENDIX B
Ten Tips for Becoming a Better Leader

We asked students and leadership coaches to share with us their best learning practices for becoming a better leader. We combined their observations with our own and others' research and summarized these lessons into the following ten tips. Think about how these apply to your own leadership development journey.

TIP 1: BE SELF-AWARE

The best leaders are highly aware of what's going on inside of them as they are leading. They're also very aware of the impact they're having on others. Think about it this way. Let's say you start falling behind in a class. You tell yourself you can catch up easily, so you ignore a couple of low grades on spot quizzes. Then one day you realize that the midterm is coming up and you haven't cracked a book in weeks. That you ignored the work for so long is going to cost you a lot in terms of time and grades.

The same is true in leading. Self-awareness gives you clues about what's going on inside you and in your environment. If you ignore those clues, you might find it difficult or impossible to catch up.

Your feelings are messages that are trying to teach you something. So, listen and learn, take time to reflect on your experiences, and keep a journal. As you go through your developmental experiences, look within yourself and pay attention to how you're feeling.

TIP 2: MANAGE YOUR EMOTIONS

The best leaders are careful not to let their feelings manage them. Instead, they manage their feelings.

Let's say that you tend to get angry when people come unprepared for a meeting. You could express your anger and put them down in front of the group. But would that be the best way to handle the situation? Common sense says that it wouldn't. The better choice would be to be aware of your anger, acknowledge it, and then decide on the most effective way to deal with the problem. The same is true in learning.

Sometimes you will feel frustrated and upset by the feedback that you receive. You might even feel angry at the person who gave you the feedback. Be aware of your feelings, but don't let them rule your behavior. If you sense that you need help managing your emotions, seek it from a trusted teacher, advisor, counselor, family member, or cleric.

TIP 3: SEEK FEEDBACK

The best leaders ask for feedback from others—feedback not only about what they're doing well but about what they're not doing well. That's one reason why managing your emotions is so important. No one is going to give you negative feedback if you're likely to get angry. Let people know that you genuinely want their feedback, and then do something with the feedback they give you. Afterward, ask, "How'd I do?" Have a conversation. Then say thanks.

TIP 4: TAKE THE INITIATIVE

The Leadership Challenge research is clear on this point: the best leaders don't wait for someone else to tell them what to do. They take the initiative to find and solve problems and to meet and create challenges. The same is true in learning: the best leaders take charge of their own learning. Because they're self-aware and seek feedback, they know their strengths and weaknesses, and they know what they need to learn. They find a way to get the experience, example, or education they need. It's your learning, your life. Take charge of it.

TIP 5: SEEK HELP

Top athletes, musicians, and performing artists all have coaches. Leadership is a performing art too, and it never hurts to have some help. Ask a teacher or mentor you respect to watch you perform, give you feedback, offer suggestions for improvement, and give you support generally. In your school or organization, there is an abundance of people you could ask to help coach you. Look to your group advisors, teachers, and faculty members you feel connected to; career centers and counseling centers might offer personal development services too. You can also consider fellow students and friends whom you feel have great leadership experiences. If you are employed, consider a coworker or supervisor. You might find yourself working with a couple of coaches who have expertise in different areas you want to explore.

TIP 6: SET GOALS AND MAKE A PLAN

If you have a clear sense of what you want to accomplish, you'll be much more likely to apply what you learn. Leaders who are successful at bringing out the best in themselves and in others set achievable stretch goals—goals that are high but not so far out of reach that people give up even before they start.

It's also important to make your goals public. You will work harder to improve when you've told others what you're trying to accomplish.

Once you've set goals, make a plan. There may be several ways to get from where you are to where you want to be, just as there are several routes you could take to travel across the country. Pick the one that best suits your needs.

When you make your plan, remember that journeys are completed one step at a time. It's the same with leadership development. You may have a strong desire to improve in three of The Five Practices of Exemplary Leadership and in ten of the thirty behaviors. That's terrific, but don't try to do everything at once. Take it bit by bit. There is no such thing as overnight success in becoming an exemplary leader.

TIP 7: PRACTICE, PRACTICE, PRACTICE

People who practice often are more likely to become experts at what they do than those who don't practice or do so only fitfully. We know this is true in the arts and in sports, but the same idea hasn't always been applied to leadership.

Practice is essential to learning. Practice might be rehearsing a speech or a new way of running a meeting. It might be sitting down with a friend to try out a conversation you plan to have with a member of your group.

Whatever it is, practice gives you the chance to become comfortable with and try out new methods, behaviors, and strategies in a safe environment. In fact, every experience is a form of practice, even when it's for real. Whether the experience is a raving success or a miserable failure, ask yourself and those involved, "What went well? What went poorly?" "What did I do well? What did I do poorly?" "What could I improve?" The best leaders are the best learners, and learning can occur at any time and anywhere.

TIP 8: MEASURE PROGRESS

You need to know whether you're making progress or marking time. It's not enough to know that you want to make it to the summit and how to recognize that summit once you're there. You also need to know whether you're still climbing or sliding downhill.

Measuring progress is crucial to improvement no matter what the activity—strengthening endurance, shedding pounds, or becoming a better leader. The best measurement systems are ones that are visible and instant—like the speedometer on your dashboard or the watch on your wrist. For instance, you can count how many thank-you notes you send out by keeping a log. A self-monitoring system can include asking for feedback. Another way to monitor your progress is to take the Student LPI more than once.

TIP 9: REWARD YOURSELF

Connect your performance to rewards. It's nice when others recognize you for your efforts, but that doesn't always happen. So along with the goals that you set and the measurement system that you put in place, create some ways to reward yourself for achieving your goals. Give yourself a night off to go to a movie or a party with a friend. Buy yourself something you'd like; it doesn't have to be expensive. Mark the achievement in red pen on your calendar. Brag about it.

You can also schedule rewards when you reach milestones. Having a learning buddy is much like how endurance sports training program Team in Training helps people prepare to run marathons and triathlons to raise money for blood cancers.

TIP 10: BE HONEST WITH YOURSELF AND HUMBLE WITH OTHERS

We know from The Leadership Challenge research that credibility is the foundation of leadership and honesty is at the top of the list of what constituents look for in a leader. But what does honesty have to do with learning to lead? Everything. The ongoing research has yet to produce a leader who scores a perfect 30 on every leadership practice. Everyone can improve, and the first step is understanding, and acknowledging, what needs improving.

Being honest means that you're willing to admit mistakes, own up to your faults, and be open to suggestions for improvement. It also means that you're accepting of the same in others.

Honesty with yourself and others produces a level of humility that earns you credibility. People don't respect know-it-alls, especially when the know-it-all doesn't know it all. Admitting mistakes and being open to new ideas and new learning communicates that you are willing to grow. It promotes a culture of honesty and openness that's healthy for you and for others.

Hubris, that is, excessive pride, is the killer disease in leadership. It's fun to be a leader, gratifying to have influence, and exhilarating when people cheer your every word. But it's easy to be seduced by power and importance. Humility is the only way to resolve the conflicts and contradictions of leadership. Excessive pride can be avoided only if you recognize that you're human and need the help of others. That in itself is an important reason for leaders being great learners.

ACKNOWLEDGMENTS

Of all the leadership lessons we have learned over the years, the one that most needs repeating at the end of a project is this one: "You can't do it alone." Leadership is not a solo performance; it's a collaborative effort. And so is writing, editing, and producing a guide such as this one. We—Jim, Barry, Beth, and Gary—couldn't have done this without the expertise, dedication, and caring of the wonderful team of exceptional people who made this possible.

First off, the only reason we were able to create the *Student Workbook and Personal Leadership Journal* is because of the gracious support of our good colleagues in colleges, universities, secondary schools, and community organizations who have dedicated themselves to developing emerging leaders. Their commitment to student leadership is inspiring, and their acceptance of our research, content, and methods has truly encouraged our hearts. We gratefully acknowledge the administrators, educators, and students who contributed their creative ideas and personal stories to this guide and to our understanding of the dynamics of leadership in their settings.

We've enjoyed a three-decades-long partnership with our publisher, Jossey-Bass, an imprint of John Wilcy & Sons. We've been a team since the beginning, and it's always a great joy to collaborate with them.

A very loud shout-out goes to our editor, Erin Null. Erin has been the champion of all *The Student Leadership Challenge* materials, and she is continuously encouraging and driving us to improve how we present our work. Erin made this revised edition happen, and she has been our guiding star on this project. Paul Foster, vice president and publisher of the Jossey-Bass higher education team, and Debra Hunter, president of Jossey-Bass and Pfeiffer imprints, have been constant sponsors of this work. Without them, we wouldn't have the resources to go from concept to distribution.

Other key members of the Jossey-Bass Higher Education Team were instrumental to the successful completion of this work. Alison Knowles, assistant editor, Bev Miller, copyeditor, and Cathy Mallon, content manager, skillfully navigated this guide through each iteration, making important improvements along the way. Others at Jossey-Bass were key to bringing this book into, and through, production and to the market. We offer our special thanks to Adrian Morgan, cover designer, and Aneesa Davenport, marketing manager, for their contributions in creating a product that others would want to open and use. For many years now, Leslie Stephen has been the developmental editor on many of our books. She brings clarity and focus to our writing, and she challenges us, directly and indirectly, to improve what we say and how we say it. We truly appreciate how she makes everything she touches better.

At the beginning of each day when we begin our work and at the end of the day when we shut down the computer for a little rest, it's our families who are there to share their love and support. We are blessed with their generous encouragement, helpful feedback, and constructive coaching. Jim and Barry are two very lucky guys to have extraordinary partners in Tae Kouzes and Jackie Schmidt-Posner. They also want to thank Nicholas Lopez, Jim's stepson; Amanda Posner, Barry's daughter; and Darryl Collins, Barry's son-in-law, for the inspiration and perspective they've provided. Beth thanks her husband, Tom, daughter, Georgia, and son, Evan, for their patience and support. Gary thanks Savannah, Sheri, Dell, and God for the support and inspiration to be a part of writing this book with Jim, Barry, and Beth.

With all these very special people in our lives, it drives home how true it is that leadership is an affair of the heart.

ABOUT THE AUTHORS

Jim Kouzes and Barry Posner have been working together for more than thirty years, studying leaders, researching leadership, conducting leadership development seminars, and serving as leaders themselves in various capacities. They are coauthors of the award-winning, best-selling book *The Leadership Challenge*. Since its first edition in 1987, *The Leadership Challenge* has sold more than 2 million copies worldwide and is available in more than twenty languages. It has been on the best-seller lists of *Business Week*, *Fortune*, and Amazon.com, and received numerous awards, including the Critics' Choice Award from the nation's book review editors, the James A. Hamilton Award for the outstanding management or health care book of the year, selected as one of the top ten books on leadership in Jack Covert and Todd Sattersten's *Top 100 Business Books of All Time*, and *FAST COMPANY* made it one of its top dozen business books of 2012.

Jim and Barry have coauthored more than a dozen other award-winning leadership books, including *Credibility: How Leaders Gain and Lose It, Why People Demand It*; *The Truth About Leadership: The No-Fads, Heart-of-the-Matter Facts You Need to Know*; *A Leader's Legacy*; *Encouraging the Heart*; *The Student Leadership Challenge*; and *The Academic Administrator's Guide to Exemplary Leadership*. They also developed the highly acclaimed Leadership Practices Inventory (LPI), a 360-degree questionnaire for assessing leadership behavior that is one of the most widely used leadership assessment instruments in the world, along with The Student LPI. The five Practices of Exemplary Leadership model they developed has been the basis of more than six hundred doctoral dissertations and academic research projects (a summary of these is available at www.theleadershipchallenge .com/research).

Among the honors and awards that Jim and Barry have received is the American Society for Training and Development's highest award for their Distinguished Contribution to Workplace Learning and Performance. They have been named Management/Leadership

Educators of the Year by the International Management Council; ranked by *Leadership Excellence* magazine in the top twenty on its list of the Top 100 Thought Leaders; named among the Top 50 Leadership Coaches in the nation (according to *Coaching for Leadership*); and listed among *HR Magazine*'s Most Influential Thinkers in the World.

Jim and Barry are frequent speakers, and each has conducted leadership development programs for organizations such as Apple, Applied Materials, ARCO, AT&T, Australia Institute of Management, Australia Post, Bank of America, Bose, Charles Schwab, Cisco Systems, Clorox, Community Leadership Association, Conference Board of Canada, Consumers Energy, Deloitte Touche, Dorothy Wylie Nursing Leadership Institute, Dow Chemical, Egon Zehnder International, Federal Express, Genentech, Google, Gymboree, HP, IBM, Jobs DR-Singapore, Johnson & Johnson, Kaiser Foundation Health Plans and Hospitals, Intel, Itau Unibanco, L.L. Bean, Lawrence Livermore National Labs, Lucile Packard Children's Hospital, Merck, Motorola, NetApp, Northrop Grumman, Novartis, Nvidia, Oakwood Housing, Oracle, Petronas, Roche Bioscience, Siemens, 3M, Toyota, United Way, USAA, Verizon, VISA, the Walt Disney Company, and Westpac. They have lectured at over sixty college and university campuses around the globe.

More information about Jim and Barry and their work, research, and services can be found at www.theleadershipchallenge.com.

• • •

James M. Kouzes is the Dean's Executive Fellow of Leadership, Leavey School of Business, at Santa Clara University, and lectures on leadership around the world to corporations, governments, and nonprofits. He is a highly regarded leadership scholar and an experienced executive; the *Wall Street Journal* has cited him as one of the twelve best executive educators in the United States. In 2010, Jim received the Thought Leadership Award from the Instructional Systems Association, the most prestigious award given by the trade association of training and development industry providers. In 2006, he received the Golden Gavel, the highest honor awarded by Toastmasters International.

Jim served as president, CEO, and chairman of The Tom Peters Company from 1988 through 1999 and prior to that led the Executive Development Center at Santa Clara University (1981–1987). He founded the Joint Center for Human Services Development at San Jose State University (1972–1980) and was on the staff of the School of Social Work, University of Texas. His career in training and development began in 1969 when he conducted seminars for Community Action Agency staff and volunteers in the war on poverty. Following graduation from Michigan State University (BA with honors in political science), he served as a Peace Corps volunteer (1967–1969). Jim can be reached at jim@kouzes.com.

• • •

Barry Z. Posner is the Michael J. Accolti, S.J., Endowed Professor of Leadership at the Leavey School of Business, Santa Clara University, where he served as dean of the school for twelve years (1997–2009). He has been a distinguished visiting professor at Hong Kong University of Science and Technology, Sabanci University (Istanbul), and the University of Western Australia. At Santa Clara, he has received the President's Distinguished Faculty Award, the school's Extraordinary Faculty Award, and several other teaching and academic honors. An internationally renowned scholar and educator, Barry is the author or coauthor of more than one hundred research and practitioner-focused articles. He currently serves on the editorial advisory boards for *Leadership and Organizational Development Journal* and the *International Journal of Servant-Leadership*. In 2011, he received the Outstanding Scholar Award from the *Journal of Management Inquiry*.

Barry received his BA (with honors) in political science from the University of California, Santa Barbara; his MA in public administration from The Ohio State University; and his PhD in organizational behavior and administrative theory from the University of Massachusetts. Having consulted with a wide variety of public and private sector organizations around the globe, Barry also works at a strategic level with a number of community-based and professional organizations, currently sitting on the board of directors of EMQ FamiliesFirst and the Global Women's Leadership Network. He has served previously on the boards of the American Institute of Architects, Big Brothers/Big Sisters of Santa Clara County, Center for Excellence in Nonprofits, Junior Achievement of Silicon Valley and Monterey Bay, Public Allies, San Jose Repertory Theater, Sigma Phi Epsilon Fraternity, and several start-up companies. Barry can be reached at bposner@scu.edu.

• • •

Beth High is an author, organizational consultant, program designer, coach, keynote speaker, and Certified Master Facilitator. Her work in these areas has allowed her to develop a strong client list from a variety of sectors, including Capital One; Girls, Inc.; John Wiley and Sons, England and Dubai; KalTire Canada; North Carolina Department of Transportation; SAS and SAS Asia Pacific; Saudi Arabia Ministry of Education; Western Union; University of Arkansas; University of North Carolina School of Government; University of North Carolina School of Business; and VF Jeanswear. She is president of High Road Consulting, a leadership development company based in Chapel Hill, North Carolina.

She has produced the Leadercast Series, a podcast series with authors Jim Kouzes and Barry Posner, and developed a Jossey-Bass Certification Program for educators interested in developing programs based on The Student Leadership Challenge. The unique blended learning approach for this program allowed Beth to create the platform on which The Leadership Challenge Workshop Online® was subsequently created. This work resulted in the creation of her partner company, HRCPartners, which focuses solely on the development and implementation of The Leadership Challenge Workshop Online and the FollowThruOnline product platforms.

Beth regularly delivers The Leadership Challenge® Workshop in a variety of formats and consults with companies globally on how to incorporate The Five Practices model into their existing leadership programs. Having completed an M.ED. in instructional design and educational media at the University of North Carolina, Chapel Hill, she is committed to top quality design of programs that explore new technologies while addressing the unique learning and development needs of the audience. Her expertise enables her to consult, design, and deliver long-format programs, lasting from eighteen to twenty-four months, built around virtual centers and using a blended learning approach. Beth and her team work closely with clients to customize program content and capture the appropriate data these sites provide. These centers allow participants to have the extended practice essential for building skills and provide the program owners with evidence of return on investment from the training. Beth can be reached at highroadconsulting@gmail.com.

• • •

Gary M. Morgan has taught or developed student leadership courses and programs at universities of all sizes for the past twenty years. He has served as a dean, director, and faculty member at campuses with enrollments ranging from twelve hundred to fifty-three thousand students and directed programs or services in student leadership, student activities and programming, student government, Greek life, residence life, orientation, the student union, judicial affairs, graduate schools and graduate student life, volunteer and community services, and many other areas. He has always held positions that had a focus on developing students as leaders. In addition to his college-level work, he has developed leadership education programs for high school students in Upward Bound and recently created a summer-long leadership program for foster youth for an Orlando, Florida, community organization.

Gary received a bachelor of science degree in communication studies (radio/TV/film) from Northern Illinois University and a master of arts degree in higher education–college student personnel from Bowling Green State University. He completed the doctoral course work and exam requirements for the Ph.D. in higher education administration at the University of South Carolina. He is a certified facilitator for The Leadership Challenge™ and Student Leadership Challenge™ and is the founder and CEO of the Student Leadership Excellence Academy and the Leadership Excellence Academy. He is a member of the American College Personnel Association, Student Affairs Administrators in Higher Education, American Society for Training and Development, International Leadership Association, and the National Clearinghouse for Leadership Programs. Gary can be contacted at gary@student-leader.com.